DATE DUE

Understanding Marxism

Understanding Marxism

An Approach through Dialogue

W. H. C. EDDY

with an introduction by
EUGENE KAMENKA

Rowman and Littlefield
Totowa, New Jersey

First published in the United States 1979 by
Rowman and Littlefield, Totowa, New Jersey

Library of Congress Cataloging in Publication Data

Eddy, William Henry Charles, 1913–1973.
 Understanding Marxism.

 Originally written as a discussion course for the Dept. of
Adult Education, University of Sydney, New South Wales.
 Bibliography: p. 148.
 1. Marx, Karl, 1818–1883. 2. Dialectical materialism. 3.
Communism and society. I. Title.
B3305.M74E33 1978   335.4′1   78–10609
ISBN 0–8476–6125–3

Printed in Great Britain

Contents

Editorial Preface

I began negotiating for the publication of W. H. C. Eddy's book in 1971. As Professor Kamenka indicates in his Introduction, the author had intended adding a discussion on more recent discussions and interpretations of Marx. This was not to be. Harry Eddy died in Sydney, Australia on 9 December 1973. Appreciative articles on various aspects of his work appeared in the W.E.A. News, the official journal of the Worker's Educational Association of New South Wales in Vol. 5, No. 1, March 1974.

Harry Eddy's untimely death led to further delays in the publication of his work. In the circumstances, an introduction became necessary. I was extremely happy to take up a suggestion by Professor Owen Harries of the School of Political Science at the University of New South Wales that the eminent scholar in Marxism Professor Eugene Kamenka be invited to write the introduction. I am extremely grateful to Professor Kamenka for his readiness to co-operate.

I am also grateful to the following for the help they gave so readily at different stages of the publication of this work. Without their ready assistance the delay in publishing Harry Eddy's essay would have been even longer: J. C. Rees, Neil Harding and H. O. Mounce of the University College of Swansea, J. L. Mackie of Oxford and, not least, Beryl Anderson of the Department of Adult Education of the University of Sydney.

Swansea, February 1978   D. Z. Phillips

Introduction

by EUGENE KAMENKA

I

Karl Marx was and remains the greatest general thinker in the history of socialism and its most powerful ideologist. Socialism as a historical movement was born in the 1830s, when men brought into relation the ideals of the French Revolution—the emphasis on liberty, equality, fraternity and human self-determination—with the miseries, class divisions and new forms of exploitation and power over men engendered by the Industrial Revolution. As a movement of, or on behalf of, the deprived and oppressed, as an intellectual protest against backwardness, superstition and 'irrational' authority and procedures, it combined disparate grievances: the traditional artisan's fear of industrialization and modern society, with their threat to his continued existence; the hatred and envy of the rich and noble that came from those millions who labour and have nothing, especially the new urban poor; the technocratic intellectual's dislike of an unplanned social system that made property, with its enormous public consequences, a private function and allowed production to continue on an individual, profit-making basis; the increasing concern of men and women of sensitivity with the social position of women; the great democratic and republican cause of those small nations whose liberty as nations was dependent upon their asserting the rights of citizens against the claims of emperors and kings ruling on the dynastic principle. The small conspiratorial cliques with which socialism began, the utopian dreams of its first exponents, the internecine quarrels and denunciations that soon broke out may now strike us as comic. But we have only to consider the fear of which the terrible June days of Paris in 1848 were born, or the bloodbath and universal detestation that accompanied the Paris commune of 1871, to know that even in the nineteenth century socialism was a movement of monumental importance whose very existence made the ruling groups and respectable classes of society tremble. By the second half of the twentieth century, we have seen the hopes and demands of those small conspiratorial groups become not only the ideologies of mass-movements and mass-parties, but almost the ideology of our time. In one form or another, socialist thinking has come to dominate most of the world.

To understand the career of socialism we must first understand the work and thought of Karl Marx. It was he who shaped and systematized the language of socialism, who synthesized—at least superficially—its conflicting hopes and aspirations, who turned socialism into an ideology, describing its place in the historical development of mankind and assuring it of a glorious and successful future. To read Marx, socialist after socialist has written, was to find one's deepest longings and aspirations given the dignity of a historical categorical imperative: it was to find that history was on your side, that the revolution must come, that mankind cannot fail.

The historical force of socialism, of course, lay in its ability to bring together diverse grievances, hopes and aspirations, to give its moral and empirical criticisms contemporary relevance and bite and, above all, to point to a seemingly simple way out. Classical Marxism has become for many thinkers *the* paradigm of an ideology—a general critique of existing society and existing conditions; a proclamation of moral and human values in terms of which these conditions are to be judged; and a mechanism, an historical, empirical description of the way in which the transition from the debased present to the glorious and moral future would be achieved. In general terms, this was the whole point of Marx's thought and life work. He began with a conception of man as an essentially or potentially autonomous, self-determined but co-operative being, capable of moulding his character, his activities and the society in which he lived in such a way as to give maximum expression to his potentialities. He began, in 1842, 1843 and 1844, to contrast this with the reality in which men actually lived—the society based on private property and the division of labour, in which men play out roles forced upon them by the impersonal logic of a system that abstracts and mystifies all human activities and institutions. He believed, from that time onward, that such human alienation and degradation had reached its peak with modern bourgeois society, which had at the same time laid enormous foundations for man's control over nature and the success of his activities. Turning from the philosophical to the economic, he strove to show, nevertheless, that bourgeois society—as part of a general pattern of historical development—carried within it the seeds of its own destruction. An economic process of enormous range and scope, but based upon private property and unplanned competition, was fraught with 'contradictions': the succession of crises, the danger of constantly recurring over-production and under-consumption, the need to make further profits at the expense of the living standard of the vast mass of humanity whose work created those profits. Capital was necessarily and not contingently intertwined with labour and could only live in constant conflict with it. As the captains of industry grew richer, more powerful and fewer, the thesis ran, the working class grew larger, relatively or absolutely poorer and more and more desperate. Finally, goaded by the misery of its conditions, in such stark contrast with the discipline and capacity engendered in the worker by the industrial process, the working class would rise, abolish private property in the means of production, distribution and exchange, overcome the abstract division of labour and the mystification of a money economy and usher in the truly human society, in which production was co-operative and for clearly recognized social purposes. Not the individual will of man, but the logic of capitalism and behind it the logic of history would bring about the social-ist/communist millennium.

This Marxian view of the world had both great power and great simplicity. It held together, with great psychological skill, a variety of contradictory beliefs—historical determinism and the belief in class struggle and the importance of individual consciousness; the affirmation of the potentially liberating effects of science and industrialization and a critique of their social effects in bourgeois society; a wistful, backward-looking elevation of the comradeship and simplicity of pre-industrial society with a clear recognition of the importance of mass political movements, centralized state power and technological development and innovation. It was thus possible for socialism to become both a radical critique of bourgeois, industrial society and, in many respects, a consummation of its values: an alternative form, in backward agrarian societies, of industrialization and modernization. The recurrent tensions in socialist movements and communist parties, the varied fortunes of the socialist ideal, the mutual recriminations and denunciations among socialists and among communists, are best understood in these terms: in seeing socialism and Marxism as a complex ideology, not unlike Christianity, which in the light of particular historical circumstances seeks to bring together, for specific social purposes and aims, disparate longings and discontents and which finds, of course, that in different circumstances and different times, these threaten to burst apart once again.

While Marx was an ideologist of extraordinary skill and power, he was also very much more than that. In ambition certainly, and in performance significantly, he was one of the great Victorians—a man seeking to systematize and bring into relation with each other all the significant fields of knowledge and thinking of his day, to gain a general view of the development of history, society and man. As an economist of the Ricardian school, he was learned and perceptive; as a student of the European politics of his time, he was no doubt biased but extremely intelligent; as a philosopher, he had a sharp eye for the requirements of logical clarity and consistency. He was, in his life and in his writing, philosopher, social scientist, political propagandist and revolutionist in one—but he understood perfectly well the difference between the various roles and he was not betrayed into simple stupidity or empty moralizing. His work, though virtually all of it that matters is either polemical or incomplete, proceeds at an extraordinary variety of levels—mingling specific insights with general theories and displaying, time and time again, a remarkable capacity to assimilate and digest the best knowledge of his day.

Karl Marx stands unequivocally with the great students of modern society, the great figures that launched contemporary social science and social theory. He stands, I believe, at the beginning of the study of modern society and not at the end. His political hopes and ambitions distort his perception; so does his temporal location, the intellectual climate, Eurocentric, evolutionist, progressivist—in which he lived. But the study of modern society in a macro-sociological way begins with him; even if his answers are false, his questions are always significant. If we wish to understand the contemporary world, we cannot circumvent Karl Marx and the systems invented in his name.

II

The study of Marx and Marxism, then, is of great intellectual (and therefore practical) importance. It is a *sine qua non* for the understanding of the modern world and of much modern thought. It is also very difficult, and like most great intellectual enterprises can never be brought to a definitive completion. The ambitions of Marx and of most Marxists have been boundless: history, philosophy, politics and economics, what man and society are, anywhere in the world, and what they will be, are all grist to the Marxist mill, questions on which they seek a comprehensive and penetrating view. Such ambitions would be ludicrous from the very beginning, before the enterprise was even commenced, if those embarked upon it did not believe that they had found a special method or key that unlocked for them the course of history and the nature of society, that enabled them to see the essence behind the appearance, and to grasp, in a world of many things, the one important, central and determining thing. The consideration of this claim—so basic to the enterprise of being a convinced and confident Marxist—is a matter for the philosopher. One of the important merits of Mr. Eddy's book is that it tackles, in simple and non-technical language and mode of presentation, the central philosophical claims associated with the Marxist enterprise and the most important categories of Marx's and Marxist thought. Through the medium of that great pedagogic device introduced to the philosophical world by the Platonic Socrates—the dialogue in which the tutored, partly tutored and untutored seek truth together, in discussion—the reader is invited to consider dialectical and historical materialism, the class struggle, the Marxist theory of the State, of ideology, religion, the worker's position under capitalism and the dictatorship of the proletariat in the period of socialism, as well as the distinction between 'utopian' and 'scientific' socialism and the work of the Marxist Party. These are questions that stand at the centre of Marx's own concerns and of the doctrines and styles of thinking that have been called Marxism. They are questions that for much of the twentieth century exercised extraordinary impact upon the intellectual development of critical social thinkers everywhere. Oceans of blood, as well as ink, have been spilt over them. Yet, despite their terrible practical consequences, they involve fundamental theoretical questions: the issue between monism and pluralism, the separate issue between free will and determinism, the nature of logic, of contradiction, of the relationship of causality, the concepts of 'consciousness' and 'representation', the issue between realism and idealism in the theory of knowledge. No man could hope to examine these questions exhaustively and definitively all in the compass of one not very large book; the great merit of Mr. Eddy's approach, apart from his concern for the pedagogic virtues, is his recognition that these questions can only be handled penetratingly and convincingly in terms of a systematic and coherent philosophical position. This position Mr. Eddy sees as empirical, pluralistic and realist, based on the recognition of objectivity, independence, historicity and complexity, rejecting essences and logical simples, hierarchies and organic wholes, and claims that all knowledge is subjective or that reality can be divided into that which acts and that which is acted upon. Mr. Eddy's general philosophical position happens to be my own; I commend it to the reader.

Today there are many Marxisms. In fact, there have always been, even in the work of Marx himself, let alone in the differences of position on some questions that can be elicited from comparing specific works or formulations of positions published by Engels with the generally philosophically more cautious and subtle but often ambiguous stands taken by Marx himself. The existence of these many Marxisms has become more obvious with the considerable growth and deepening of Marx scholarship in Europe and in English-speaking lands in the period since the Second World War; it has been made dramatically evident to the world by the Yugoslav break with the Cominform, by the Sino-Soviet split, the resultant development of polycentric communism and the emergence of the New Left and of the various Eurocommunisms. Yet, the student must begin somewhere: he cannot master everything before he considers anything. It is possible to approach a study of Marxism by beginning with a careful consideration of the intellectual thrust and development of the work of Marx himself, seen as a process of self-education and self-clarification over time. This is the approach adopted, for instance, in my own *The Ethical Foundations of Marxism* or in Professor Shlomo Avineri's *The Social and Political Thought of Karl Marx*. It is possible, at the same time or alternatively, to approach Marxism as a historical ideology and not merely the thought of one man, and thus to emphasize even more strongly its role in and relation with modern European history. That is the achievement of the late Mr. George Lichtheim's *Marxism: An Historical and Critical Study*. Since those books were published, the study of Marx and Marxism has become an industry, with its inevitable multiplication of refinements, loss of imagination and comprehensive vision and pedestrianization of purpose and thrust. Not many of those who write about Marx as a philosopher today have either the philosophical competence or the philosophical independence from contemporary fashions to do it well. The most recent revival of interest in Marx and Marxism as philosophy has been a vehicle for obscurantism, for the rejection of empirical and scientific modes of thinking, for the Germanization, the Hegelianization and Fichteanization, of Gallic and Anglo-Saxon culture. Mr. Eddy's book, by contrast, focuses on those aspects of the thought of Marx and Engels that made Marxism a great and important late nineteenth and twentieth century ideology and a pretender to the role of being one of the great systems of social, philosophical and in a sense ethical thought. It provides for that reason a third way of approaching

Marx and Marxism for the beginner. It is a book for the student who wishes to understand, rather than to appear fashionable and up-to-date by parrotting scholastic commentaries and academic jargon that he cannot possibly understand without first having worked through the sorts of issues discussed by Eddy with attention to the basic simplicities that Eddy emphasizes. It is as a prophylactic against the higher illiteracy so prevalent today that I would commend Mr. Eddy's book.

III

William Henry Charles Eddy, who died in Sydney, Australia, on 9 December 1973, as President of the Workers' Educational Association of New South Wales—in which he had been active for thirty-seven years—and as Senior Lecturer in the Department of Adult Education of the University of Sydney, in charge of the Metropolitan Classes Programme, was and remains one of the most influential and respected figures in the history of adult education in Australia. His influence on the W.E.A., as tutor, committee man and office-bearer in its governing structures, was profound; the devotion and admiration of those he tutored, in Newcastle (N.S.W.) and Sydney, over thirty years is a living testament not only to his pedagogical skill and enthusiasm, but, above all, to his total commitment to the life of thought and enquiry, of criticism and discussion, and to the Socratic belief that education is a drawing out and development of the student's capacities for observation, assimilation and argument. He believed with Socrates and his own teacher at the University of Sydney, the late Professor John Anderson, that the unexamined life was not worth living, that no subjects were outside or beyond enquiry, that free thought and culture were themselves powerful and important historical traditions and ethical goods, which could not be left out of account in discussing either ethics or politics, either society or man. Like Anderson, he gave to philosophy the passion that other men associate with politics and to politics the passion that some men associate only with philosophy. He had no doubt that philosophy, as the general theory of what is, stood at the centre of all knowledge and that logic (in a modified traditional Aristotelian form) stood at the centre of philosophy, giving it a unified, systematic character. But his own special interests were largely in ethics and politics and he lived his ethics and politics as he—like most Andersonians—lived his philosophy. Marxism and social theory—from which he believed one could not divorce the distinction between goods and evils as historical social processes—absorbed much, if not most, of his life. Like many of his generation, he moved through all the personal and intellectual agonies of radical discussion in the 1930s and 1940s, from involvement in Trotskyism to a strong anti-communism, never divorced from a real sympathy for and understanding of the militantly working class steel-producing town in which he spent much of his life.

The book before the reader is a slightly edited version of the discussion course that Eddy wrote for his tutorial groups in the early 1950s and used for many years with great success to stimulate discussion and enquiry among his students. I hope it will do the same for a wider readership now. If Eddy's untimely death had not prevented this, he would have wished to add a dialogue on more recent discussions and interpretations of Marx. A year or so before his death he had read with admiration the work of another fellow-Australian and Andersonian then living in Paris, Neil McInnes' *The Western Marxists*. In reviewing that book Eddy wrote:

McInnes argues that Marx was not an epistemologist. Until I read this book I had accepted Leninist representationalism as the genuine Marxist epistemology, though recognising that it was an untenable theory. McInnes demonstrates its untenability in a compressed and powerful argument, but he also demonstrates that the theory is not Marxist. With equal force he argues against the views of Arturo Labriola and of Sidney Hook who held that the Marxist doctrine of praxis was a form of pragmatism.

More generally, Eddy's review makes it clear that he sees the New Left of the 1960s as history repeating itself in caricature form—the utopian socialism and radical humanism of the 1840s made absurd by repetition a 120 years later. He agrees with McInnes that the Critical Theory of the Frankfurt School in the 1920s picked up what was ephemeral in the early Marx's work, while paving the way for irrationalist distortions of

Marxism (and for Nazism) by treating science and technology, and even formal logic and reason, as examples of reification and domination. Thus Eddy, in the beginning of 1973, had no doubt that much of the latest 'Western Marxism' amounted to a remystification of Marx, to a retreat from his positions. But he did think too that the new Western Marxists had found some theoretical ways forward from Marx, e.g., in criticizing or rejecting his social monism.

No study of Marx or Marxism, as I have said, can be complete. There is always much more to be said. If Harry Eddy had lived, he would have said some of it, in this book and elsewhere. But what he discusses here is important and self-standing; it comes logically and historically before and not after the discussion of recent years. For the critical understanding of that discussion it is an important preliminary. Eddy himself would have wished nothing more than that his book might drive the reader on to further thinking and reading, but only after he had digested those central issues and arguments to which Eddy rightly draws attention and which he approaches with a worked-out philosophical position that provides an important safeguard against empty eclecticism and obscurantist confusion.

Canberra–London, January, 1978   Eugene Kamenka

I

Marxist Philosophy

CHAIRMAN: We are setting out to discuss certain aspects of Marxist theory but we must not imagine that, in ten discussions, we are going to do this thoroughly. Many important points in Marxist theory we shall have to leave untouched in order to concentrate on its central assertions. Even on these, it will be impossible for us to review all that is to be said either for or against.

You understand, gentlemen, what is going to happen. You three are to have ten discussions on Marxist theory. The scripts of your discussions will be circulated to members of discussion groups who will read them and discuss what you have said, trying to arrive at the truth about it. I am going to ask you to bear in mind one thing. At least two of the three of you have studied this subject. I want you to remember that many members of groups will have made no such study. What you have to say will be their introduction to the subject. So will you please take pains to be as clear as possible.

SOUTH: Mr. Chairman, if you will permit me a word. Sometimes when I am asked to be 'clear', I am really being asked to be easy. I'd like, right from the start, to make myself clear about that. We have ten discussions before us. You have set us, if I may say so, an ambitious programme. Unless we are prepared to be superficial, we can't make what we have to say easy. Most people are not familiar with Marxism or criticisms of it. They can't expect to see the force of what we have to say without thinking about it. I'll certainly do my best to be clear, but group members who don't already know Marxism, will have to work on the material if they want to gain an understanding of it.

CHAIRMAN: Quite so, but that is a matter for them. As for

you, I realize that you cannot be easier than the subject will allow. Perhaps I have made things more difficult for group members by suggesting that we begin our discussions here, by considering on the first night, 'Marxist Philosophy'. We might have made an easier beginning on 'The Class Struggle' or 'The Communist Party'. However, when the leading Marxists talk about those subjects their philosophy is one of the main roots of what they say. So I thought we might as well go directly to this root.

Before we make a beginning perhaps I had better say who we are: (I think they call it 'reading into the record'). Mr. Allen here is a Marxist. Of what school Allen—Stalinist? Trotskyist? Kautskian?

ALLEN: No, no, None of these. I am a Marxist. I stand by the doctrines of Marx and Engels. These 'schools' you speak about, have some of the Marxist doctrines but I stand by genuine Marxism.

SOUTH: I think these schools would all want to challenge you about that.

CHAIRMAN: We won't go into that now. We realize that among Marxists, there are different opinions about what Marxism is. I assume that Allen will give us quotations from Marx and Engels. Group members will be able to check up on his interpretations by reading the works of these authors. And you can challenge him yourself on any specific point where you think he is not giving an accurate interpretation of Marxism. Mr. South is a critic of Marxism. Will that be a sufficient label for you, South?

SOUTH: Hardly. Marxism is criticized from many points of view. As for my criticisms it is difficult to give one over-all label since they have many aspects. But I think 'pluralist' is as adequate as any. I hope what I mean by that will become clear as we go along.

CHAIRMAN: We hope so. Mr. Streeter claims to represent the plain man.

STREETER: That is so. I mean that I don't claim to know anything about Marxism except what I've read in the papers. I don't expect to be able to contribute anything positive to the discussion but perhaps I can ask some useful questions. Anyway that is what you asked me to come and do, and I'll try.

CHAIRMAN: Good. Then we all know roughly where we stand—Allen a Marxist, South a pluralist critic of Marxism, Streeter a plain man. And we are going to discuss Marxist Philosophy. Perhaps you would be the best to begin Allen. You tell us what it is. South can try to show us where he thinks it is false and Streeter can ask his questions.

ALLEN: Well . . . Marx and Engels were influenced by the German Philosopher Hegel. But they did not merely follow Hegel. They kept what was valuable in Hegel and discarded what was unsound. Hegel thought that the universe was mental. Marx and Engels saw that it was matter. Engels says that 'the real unity of the universe consists in its materiality.'

STREETER: What do the Marxists mean by 'matter'?

ALLEN: On that point they are not dogmatic. Here I think we can safely follow Lenin. In my opinion he is not a good Marxist in some of his political theories but he follows Marx and Engels very closely in his philosophy. In his philosophical work—*Materialism and Empirio-Criticism* Lenin deals with this question of the nature of matter. He is considering the views of certain physicists that 'matter disappears' for they can reduce it to electricity. Lenin does not think this undermines a materialist philosophy. It simply means that 'those properties of matter which before seemed absolute, immutable, and primary (impenetrability, inertia, mass, etc.) disappear, and now become relative, belonging only to certain states of matter.' 'The real meaning of the disappearance of matter' is that 'the natural sciences lead to the "unity of matter".' You can see that Lenin regards it as unimportant what properties, at any given time, are attributed to matter. What scientists once thought to be absolute properties of matter, they may come to find belong only to certain states of matter. That is simply a question of scientific progress. The important thing is that matter is there. As he says—'. . . the sole "property" of matter—with the recognition of which materialism is vitally connected—is the property of being *objective reality*, of existing outside of our cognition.'

STREETER: I think I see your main points: The unity of the universe consists in its being matter which is itself a unity. We may find out more about matter so that some of the things we now believe about it may turn out to be wrong . . .

ALLEN: Not necessarily wrong, but with only a limited truth. What used to be believed about matter was not entirely wrong. It is true of certain states of matter.

STREETER: I see. And the other point about matter—and this is the one Lenin says is vital for materialism—is that it is objective reality. But what does he mean by saying that it exists 'outside of our cognition'? Does he mean that we don't know it?

ALLEN: No, he does not mean that, though what he says does imply that material things do exist even if we don't happen to know them: for example, before man was on the earth, it did exist, it had objective reality.

STREETER: Surely that is obvious. Who would deny that?

ALLEN: Lenin himself points out that there are two possible lines of theory. 'All knowledge,' he says, 'is derived from experience, from sensation, from perception. But the question remains, is the source of perception, objective reality? If you answer affirmatively, then you are a materialist. If not, then you inevitably come to subjectivism. . . .'

STREETER: Subjectivism?

ALLEN: Yes, the doctrine that our knowledge is subjective, that it is true for us. If you deny that objective reality is the source of our perceptions then you have no alternative but to say that those perceptions are purely subjective. A little earlier Lenin has said that 'starting from sensations, it is theoretically possible to follow the line of subjectivism which leads to solipsism ("bodies are complexes or combinations of sensations"), or to follow the line of objectivism which leads to materialism ("sensations are images of objects in the external world").' For the first viewpoint, he says, 'there cannot be any objective truth', whereas for the second viewpoint, for materialism, 'the recognition of the objective truth is essential.'

STREETER: I see. There is still one point I would like cleared up. Lenin says, 'it is theoretically possible to follow the line of subjectivism . . . or to follow the line of objectivism which leads to materialism.' Does he mean that you can't settle this question, that you simply have a choice?

ALLEN: That is correct. You can't settle the question theoretically, you can't settle it by argument. You can see that this must be so if we start from our sensations, as we must; they are all that we have. If in any of our perceptions we can't get past our sensations, how can we settle whether objects are simply the product of our minds rather than the external sources which produce our sensations? How can we settle that theoretically? We can't do it. Lenin admits that a thinker like Berkeley who argues the subjectivist case can't be answered. At the same time Berkeley can't answer the materialist.

STREETER: But that is no good. That is just a stalemate. Whether you become a materialist or not is simply an act of faith.

ALLEN: Speaking purely theoretically, yes. But you have to remember an important point Marx made about this. In his second thesis on Feuerbach he wrote. 'The question whether objective truth can be attributed to human thinking is not a question of theory but is a practical question. In practice man must prove the truth . . . of his thinking.' It was because he was engaged in a certain kind of practice that Marx was able to see and be convinced by materialism, and reject the idealism of Hegel—i.e. the view that reality is idea which is dependent on being known.

CHAIRMAN: I think we have gone far enough for the present. I know that South will want to subject what Allen has had to say to a critical examination.

SOUTH: Let me make it clear that I am not going to criticize from an idealist or a subjectivist point of view. If anyone wants to consider the arguments from that side, he can read Berkeley's *Treatise Concerning the Principles of Human Knowledge*. I am not an idealist and I think the Marxists were right when they explicitly rejected idealism. If materialism were used to mean no more than that there is an objective reality which is not dependent on mind, then I should describe myself as a materialist. But I think it can be shown that idealism is unsound; I think Berkeley can be answered.

STREETER: You mean theoretically.

SOUTH: Yes, I mean theoretically. In order to deny objective truth, in order to state his theory, (or even to recognise it—which comes to the same thing) a thinker has to assert that it is objectively true. If he says that we know only our own sensations or only ideas then he is saying that this is objectively true, that it is in fact so, whatever we may happen to think about it. In other words in order to state the theory it is necessary to proceed upon the assumption that the theory is false. That in itself is enough to demolish the theory.

STREETER: But that does not show that trees and clouds and things in general exist.

SOUTH: No, it does not. But it does make good the case for objective reality. However I want to come on to the points where I disagree with the Marxist conclusions. I agree with them that there is objective reality, I agree with them in rejecting the view that spirit is primary, nature secondary and dependent on spirit. But I disagree with their view that nature is matter and that this gives it its unity.

STREETER: What are you going to substitute? You deny that spirit is primary, now you are denying that matter is primary. What do you say is primary?

SOUTH: I deny that anything is primary. It is no accident that Engels and Lenin cannot say what matter is. You couldn't have science if there were a unity of the universe whether that unity is supposed to consist in its being matter, being spirit or being anything else. Parmenides made that clear long ago. Suppose for the sake of argument, that we accept the Marxist position that all reality is matter. Then we can have no history, no change. To have change we should have to have one form of matter replacing another form of matter. Yet the first form and the second form must each be simply matter. If they are not, then it is not true that all reality is matter. If they are, then the first form and the second form are the same and there has been no change. So you have to give up the theory that reality is One or you give up the theory that there is change.

STREETER: That does not sound right to me. Aren't you assuming that there is a change in substance between the first form and the second form? Couldn't it be true that the stuff remained the same but (let us say) the shape changed?

SOUTH: I don't see any difference in principle. But I'll follow up your argument and see where it leads us. Suppose the stuff remained the same and the shape changed. Isn't the shape real? You had a sphere of matter and now you have a cube of matter. You can't say that the spherical shape and the cuboid shape are each merely matter. If you did you'd be denying that there was any difference between them. Here already you have broken up the unity of reality. There is not simply one thing but at least three. And of course there are other shapes. And the same sort of argument applies to what you call substance. Wood can become coal. There are properties of wood that are not properties of coal and there are properties of coal that are not properties of wood. We couldn't distinguish between them if this were not so. If you were going to say that wood and coal are merely matter then you would be denying any distinction between them.

STREETER: I see what you're driving at. All the same, may it not be true that if you analysed wood and coal far enough you'd find that basically they were made of only one ingredient—an ingredient common to both.

SOUTH: It is impossible to show how with one ingredient and one alone you can get two different things. But even if we forget that, even if we assume that wood and coal each have only one ingredient, namely matter, it remains a fact that the wood and coal exist. They have their own properties as wood and as coal. They are real. Even if there is such a thing as matter it is not exactly the same as wood and coal. (It can't be exactly the same as both for they are different.) Unless you are prepared to recognize the reality of many things you can't have a coherent theory, you can't have science. And we can observe many things with various characters. That is why I say that pluralism is a sound theory, that attempts to reduce reality to One, or Monism as it is called, are bound to break down. The Marxist theory of matter is no exception. Marx and Engels thought they were making an advance when they threw out the notions of idea, spirit, or mind as the One, and substituted the notion of matter. They thought they were throwing out the supernatural. In fact it made no difference. They might as well have filled in X as matter. All such theories are open to the same criticism.

STREETER: Then where do you fit in mind or spirit? You said, didn't you, that you reject the view that spirit is primary, nature secondary. In that you agreed with the Marxists.

SOUTH: Yes, but I disagree with Engels' and Lenin's materialism when they say that 'to the materialists nature is primary and spirit secondary.' For the theory I have been putting forward minds or spirits exist, are real, are in fact there just as are clouds and trees. Indeed you can put it this way—minds are a part of nature—as long as you remember that 'nature' does not mean simply one thing. Minds have qualities and ways of acting in common with other things and they also have their own peculiarities in virtue of which we are able to distinguish them as minds. We could say the same about trees or anything else.

CHAIRMAN: Is that all, South?

SOUTH: I realize I've used up my time and I'd like to take up many other points. I'll confine myself to this matter of proving the truth of a theory by practice. I'll be brief. First, successful practice is no proof of theory. A witch doctor might hold the theory that certain types of diseases are due to an offended god. He might prescribe ritual bathing and the offering up of certain sacrifices for purification. And his cures may work as well as those based on a more scientific approach. What may be needed is cleanliness and psychological influence. These the witch doctor supplies though his reasons are all wrong. And no amount of successful practice can prove his reasons right.

This is only a particular illustration of the general position. Practice teaches us nothing except insofar as we theorize about it. We have to observe results, observe the connection between results and their causes. In other words it is by means of theory that we are testing theory. We are observing what is the case. We can do this about our own practice of course. But we can also simply observe without ourselves indulging in any practice about the matter apart from observation. So theory not practice is the test of theory even though sometimes the testing is by means of theory about practice.

CHAIRMAN: Thank you, South. I should now be able to pose some of the issues. Members of groups might like to look further into them.

1. Allen and South agree that there is objective reality, reality not dependent on the mind, on being known. Various thinkers of whom Berkeley is one, disagree. Who is right? Why?

2. South thinks that those who disagree can be answered. He has attempted to sketch an answer. Allen agrees with Lenin

in thinking the issue cannot be settled theoretically. Can it be settled or not? If so, how? If not, why not?

3. The Marxists think that matter is what gives unity to the universe. South denies unity, thinks any such theory must break down. Only a pluralist theory can be coherent.

Is South right? If he is not, is the Marxist theory any advance on other monistic theories or not?

4. Is practice *the* test of the truth of theory or not?

These are some issues that can be further discussed. There are several others. But you have more to say about Marxist Philosophy, Allen?

ALLEN: I certainly have. South here, has been trying to show that a Monist theory like materialism involves certain contradictions. He also asserts that it can give no account of history. I'm afraid I can't regard his criticisms as decisive. Marxism has a great deal to say about contradictions and also it is the only scientific theory of history. It would be a strange fact if a theory, on a philosophical basis (materialism) inconsistent with history, should turn out to throw a flood of light on history. Yet that is what Marxism does. So there must be something wrong with South's argument. I will tell you exactly what it is. He has remembered that Marxism is materialism but he has forgotten that it is dialectical materialism. He has forgotten the dialectic!

STREETER: He has forgotten the dialectic? What is the dialectic and how does that affect the position?

ALLEN: The dialectic removes our worries about contradictions, it gives us the key to the understanding of history, and it shows how there is progress from lower to higher.

STREETER: It sounds like an important theory.

ALLEN: It certainly is. Whoever does not understand the dialectic misses something that is of central importance in Marxism. I have not the time to expound it fully here. I can give merely a sketch. If you want to study it more fully you can do so in three works by Engels—*Ludwig Feuerbach, Anti-Duhring,* and *Dialectics of Nature*. There is also a short but suggestive note at the back of Lenin's *Materialism and Empirio-Criticism.*

Marx and Engels did not discover the dialectic. They took it over from Hegel and it has a considerable history before

Hegel, but we will not go into that now. As it appears in
Hegel, the theory is of a dialectic of ideas or concepts. Suppose
we assume a certain concept (the thesis); this begets its opposite or negation (the antithesis); the contradiction between
thesis and antithesis is resolved by a third concept (the synthesis) which transcends the first two but at the same time
preserves them at a higher level. This was the Hegelian dialectic. The trouble with this self-movement of the concept was,
as Engels says, that it was going on 'no one knows where.'
Nevertheless, in spite of the mystification with which it was
mixed up, the dialectic of Hegel contained something valuable. By Marx and Engels it 'was placed upon its head; or
rather turned off its head, on which it was standing before, and
placed upon its feet again.'

STREETER: Well, it may be true that the dialectic makes
many things clear, but I'm still not clear about the dialectic
itself.

ALLEN: This is what Marx and Engels did. They 'comprehended the concepts in (their) heads once more
materialistically—as images of real things . . .' Then it was
possible to take the dialectic as 'the science of the general laws
of motion—both of the external world and of human
thought.'

STREETER: Look, you'll have to give me an example. I don't
get hold of this at all.

ALLEN: Well the most famous Marxist example is that of
the class struggle. We find wealth, private property in the
means of production, this begets its negation, its opposite—propertylessness or the proletariat. Here we have the
thesis and the antithesis. But the negation is itself negated in
the revolution and the coming of the classless society which
brings to an end not only private property but also the proletariat as an exploited propertyless class. Yet property is
preserved in this third phase (or synthesis) but at a higher level.
It is social property. Similarly the seed becomes the plant
which in turn returns to seed—but this time many seeds. You
will find many other examples in Engels.

STREETER: I see. And while these things happen in the
external world, there is a dialectic also in the mind, among
ideas which are copies of the external world?

ALLEN: That is correct. Now you will notice certain important aspects of dialectical materialism. Dialectic means that 'the world is not to be comprehended as a complex of ready-made *things*, but as a complex of *processes*, in which the things apparently stable no less than their mind-images in our heads, the concepts, go through an uninterrupted change of coming into being and passing away . . .'. The dialectic recognizes a dynamic not a static world.

Secondly, since each synthesis becomes a new thesis with its own negation and then the final resolution of that contradiction in a new synthesis, that 'uninterrupted change of coming into being and passing away' of which I have already spoken is one 'in which, in spite of all seeming accidents and of all temporary retrogression, a progressive development asserts itself in the end . . .'

Thirdly the dialectic enables us both to recognize and to reconcile contradictions. As Lenin says, 'The division of the One and the knowledge of its contradictory parts' . . . '*is* the essence . . . of dialectics.' There are contradictions in things and it is a merit of the dialectic that it recognizes this fact.

STREETER: Just a minute. I can't have that. You say that there are contradictions in things. You can't show me that straight both is and is not crooked, or any similar contradiction.

ALLEN: I'm glad you used that example because Engels uses it himself when he is replying to Duhring who also thinks 'there are no contradictions in things'. What Engels says is this: 'This statement will have for people of average common sense the same self-evident truth as to say that straight cannot be crooked nor crooked straight. But the differential calculus shows in spite of all the protests of common sense that under certain conditions straight and crooked are identical, and reaches thereby a conclusion which is not in harmony with the common sense view of the absurdity of there being any identity between straight and crooked.' And Engels goes on to show that you have the same sort of contradiction involved in motion. 'Motion is itself a contradiction since simple mechanical movement from place to place can only accomplish itself by a body being at one and the same moment in one place and simultaneously in another place, by being in one and the same place and yet not there. And motion is just the continuous establishing and dissolving the contradiction.' And Engels gives many other examples of contradictions in things. Dialectic recognizes them and in this lies its superiority to other theories. All development is by a process of contradiction and the dissolving of the contradiction. Theories that try to deny contradiction simply condemn themselves to barrenness as far as giving an account of development is concerned.

CHAIRMAN: Well . . . there is plenty there to be discussed. Let me see if I can summarize what you have said.

1. The world is not static but dynamic. It is in continuous process.

ALLEN: Yes, and it is a complex of processes.

CHAIRMAN:

2. These processes occur in three phases—a thesis, an antithesis which is the opposite or negation of the thesis, and a synthesis which negates the antithesis but dissolves or reconciles the contradiction of thesis and antithesis and preserves features of thesis and antithesis but at a higher level.

3. Hence the world is a development upwards.

4. There are contradictions in things and the dialectic recognizes them and how, in development, they are overcome.

That combined with what you had to say about materialism would sum up Marxist Philosophy, would it, Allen?

ALLEN: There is more to it than that. We have said practically nothing about the theory of knowledge or the theory of truth or many other things for that matter. Nevertheless what you have said is the bare bones of dialectical materialism.

CHAIRMAN: Good. I'm afraid we haven't time to get past bare bones. So now I'll ask South to give us the bare bones of his criticism—that is if he wants to make any criticism.

SOUTH: I certainly do, but like Allen I can't hope to develop it fully. Those who want to go into it more thoroughly can read 'Marxism, is it Science?' by Max Eastman and an article 'Marxist Philosophy' by John Anderson in The Australasian Journal of Psychology and Philosophy, March, 1935.

My view is that the addition of the dialectic to materialism to make dialectical materialism does not help Marxists in any way to get over the difficulties in any monist theory. In fact it simply adds difficulties of its own. At almost all points it seems to me to be a mystification.

STREETER: Almost all points? Then I take it you agree with something.

SOUTH: I agree with something that Marxists have linked with the dialectic but which I believe to be quite independent of it. I think it is true that we find the dynamic not the static, that things are in process, that there are complexes of processes. That much is true but it has no necessary connection with dialectic. It is possible to hold a process theory without holding a dialectical theory. In fact you confuse a process theory by making it dialectical.

STREETER: If, as you say, a process theory is sound, how can dialectic confuse it?

SOUTH: By giving a false account of process. Take this division of process into units of three for example. That is quite an arbitrary matter. No doubt you can find processes and point to three phases. Take the life of man. You may say there is pre-maturity, maturity and post-maturity. These divisions are no doubt real. But you can also point to infancy, childhood, adolescence, young manhood, middle age and so on. You are dealing with real phases here too. We simply do not find that processes go on in sets of three phases and not in sets of four, five, two, seven or other numbers of phases.

STREETER: I see that but it is only a minor point isn't it? Are any important confusions involved in having a dialectical theory of process?

SOUTH: I don't think it is a minor point. The theory of three phases is closely tied up with this thesis—antithesis theory and that in turn with the theory of contradiction and also with the theory of an upward development—and they are all false.

STREETER: Why are they all false? Take them one at a time. Why is the thesis-antithesis theory false?

SOUTH: You can only maintain that theory by playing fast and loose with the notion of opposites, with the notion of negation. What justification is there for saying that the plant is the opposite of the seed or the negation of the seed? Certainly it differs from the seed but so does my shoe. If you say that the seed ceases to exist when the plant comes into existence then that is true, but it doesn't make the plant the opposite of the seed, and if you say it makes the plant the negation of the seed then this simply means that you are using the phrase 'negation of an earlier phase' to mean the succeeding phase.

STREETER: Couldn't you do that?

SOUTH: It is certainly not what the Marxists are doing, because it would not get them that contradiction which is such an important part of the theory. You just don't find things giving way to their opposites. You find earlier and later phases, the later having things in common with the earlier and also respects in which they differ. Any third phase will be in the same position—so will a fourth, fifth, sixth, seventh and so on.

STREETER: This seems to be an example of your pluralism.

SOUTH: Yes, it is but I am not starting with a pluralist theory and trying to impose it on the facts. I am saying that that is what we find.

STREETER: Well, what about contradiction?

SOUTH: I think that I can't do better on that than to quote from Anderson. He deals with those points about 'straight and crooked' and 'motion' that Allen was quoting from Engels. He deals with other points that Engels and Lenin make too—but we won't go into those.

STREETER: Well, let us hear what he has to say about 'straight and crooked' and the differential calculus. Allen, or rather Engels, had me baffled there with this differential calculus. I don't know anything about that. What does Anderson say about it?

SOUTH: He says—'The calculus is certainly a curious instrument in the hands of Engels; but the most that could be meant by saying that it shows that 'under certain conditions straight and crooked are identical' is that *some straight things are crooked*. Now, if this is true, it means that the commonsense view that 'straight cannot be crooked', i.e. *no straight things are crooked*, is false; it does not mean that straightness and crookedness are at once compatible and incompatible. Neither calculus nor anything else will enable Engels to prove this, which would be a real contradiction.'

STREETER: It looks as though I was right the first time. What does he say about motion?

SOUTH: He says that Engels's passage which Allen quoted . . .

is a mere misstatement . . . There is a sense in which it may be said that a thing is in two places at the same time, if its stretch covers both places, but there is no sense in which it can be said that a thing is both at a place and not there. If we seriously mean either assertion, we do not mean the other. Engels falls into the old Pythagorean confusion about 'moments' as minimum times at which something can happen; actually moments are the boundaries of durations, and while we can say that a thing is at a place *up* to a certain moment and is not there *from* that moment (in which case, of course, there is no contradiction) we cannot say that it is at a place at a moment—it is just the contradiction that would then arise that forces us to the other view . . .

STREETER: H'm. That is more difficult. It all seems to swing on the meaning of 'moment'. I think I catch his drift but I'll have to consider that one. Anyway the most important thing is not the example but the general point—'are there contradictions in things?'

SOUTH: Admittedly these are only examples that have been disposed of, nevertheless it is significant that Engels can't state coherently any example of contradiction in things. You can find the same sorts of misstatements in other examples he gives.

ALLEN: That assertion can be disputed South, but I don't want to spend time on that now. I want to come right to the crux of the matter. In the note that I mentioned Lenin quotes from Hegel who says '. . . in *every* judgement there is such a statement made as the *individual* is the *general*, or, still more definitely, *the subject is the predicate* (for instance, God is absolute spirit). No doubt the notions of individuality, universality, subject and predicate, are also quite different, but it remains none the less true in general that every judgement is really a statement of identity.' You see what Hegel is pointing out here. Subject (in his example—God) and predicate (in his example—absolute spirit) are different.

SOUTH: I see that. If they were not different we would not be saying anything. God is God does not mean anything.

ALLEN: Yet when we say God is absolute spirit we are asserting that they are the same, we are asserting identity.

Similarly if we say 'The workers are propertyless' the subject (workers) and the predicate (propertyless) are different yet in making the judgement we are asserting that they are the same. There is a contradiction there and that is in every judgement. In other words it is in all the situations that are judged. The universe is shot through with contradictions, contradiction is the moving force of its development. It is not a question of isolated examples of contradiction. The dialectic is a theory of all reality and it depends on contradiction being everywhere. If contradiction is not involved in all judgements then I agree with Lenin that would mean the dialectic is not sound. On the other hand the contradiction is plainly there in every judgement. Subject and predicate are distinct and not distinct.

SOUTH: I agree with you and Lenin that the dialectic is unsound if this argument of Hegel's breaks down. And I think it does break down. I have already agreed with you that subject and predicate are different—otherwise we are making no judgement. To use your example—if workers meant simply propertyless then we'd be saying nothing if we made that judgement. 'The workers are propertyless' would be 'The propertyless are propertyless.' That is saying nothing. It conveys no information. We agree then that there must be difference or distinction.

But I deny that in making a judgement we are identifying subject and predicate. What we are saying is that beings of a certain sort (namely workers) are also of a certain other sort (namely propertyless) and this is not an assertion of identity. You can see that, if you consider this fact: it could be true that workers are propertyless and at the same time it could be true that some propertyless are not workers. Where does your identity come in? There is much more to be said . . .

CHAIRMAN: I must ask you not to say it, South. I think you have given enough there for discussion on that point. Is there any other major point you want to make?

SOUTH: Only this point, Mr. Chairman: Once you have cut away all these foundations from the dialectic you have nothing left to sustain the theory that it is a development upwards. The upward path depends on the alleged fact that the synthesis resolves the contradictions of thesis and antithesis and reproduces their features at a higher level. I have shown that there are no contradictions in things, that you don't get this threefold phase development, that later stages are not negations of the earlier and so on. The whole case for the upward path breaks down. Whether there is an upward path or not becomes then a matter of what we find to be true. My own view is that we have not up or down outside human society. And within human history I think we find ups and downs.

II

The Theory of History

CHAIRMAN: This time I am suggesting that you discuss the Marxist theory of history. Allen, would you mind, as a Marxist, telling us what it is?

ALLEN: I'll be glad to do that. I believe Marx's theory of history to be one of the most important discoveries ever made. It is so important that I hesitate to give my statement of it; I think it would be better if I present it in Marx's own words.

CHAIRMAN: I agree that it would be valuable to have Marx's version but is there not some difficulty in following Marx's use of terms? ·

ALLEN: I have been thinking about that. What you say is true but I think we can get over the difficulty. I will quote Marx, then, if there is anything that is not clear, Streeter here can ask me about it and I'll do my best to explain. I cannot see much point in claiming to study Marxism if we are not prepared to grapple with what Marx himself has to say, no matter how difficult at first sight, it may seem to be.

CHAIRMAN: Quite so. The procedure you propose seems to me to be reasonable. What is it you will quote?

ALLEN: I think the best basis for our discussion is Marx's Summary of his theory of history in his Preface to his *A Contribution to the Critique of Political Economy*. This passage is crucial for this discussion tonight and will have an important bearing on later discussions as well.

CHAIRMAN: I agree entirely. It has always seemed to me that that statement is one of the most important in all Marxist writings. Anyone who wants to understand Marxism should study it carefully. Will you give it to us now?

ALLEN: Yes, here is the quotation. I will read it.

In the social production of their subsistence men enter into determined and necessary relations with each other which are independent of their wills—production-relations which correspond to a definite stage of development of their material productive forces. The sum of these production-relations forms the economic structure of society, the real basis upon which juridical and political superstructure arises, and to which definite social forms of consciousness correspond. The mode of production of the material subsistence, conditions the social, political and spiritual life-process in general. It is not the consciousness of men which determines their existence, but on the contrary it is their social existence which determines their consciousness. At a certain stage of their development the material productive forces of society come into contradiction with the existing production-relations, or what is merely a juridical expression for the same thing, the property relations within which they have operated before. From being forms of development of the productive forces these relations turn into fetters upon their development. Then comes an epoch of social revolution. With the change in the economic foundation the whole immense superstructure is slowly or rapidly transformed. In studying such a transformation one must always distinguish between the material transformation in the economic conditions essential to production—which can be established with the exactitude of natural science—and the juridical, political, religious, artistic or philosophic, in short ideological forms, in which men become conscious of this conflict and fight it out. As little as one judges what an individual is by what he thinks of himself, so little can one judge such an epoch of transformation by its consciousness; one must rather explain this consciousness by the contradictions in the material life, the conflict at hand between the social forces of production and the relations in which production is carried on. No social formation ever disappears before all the productive forces are developed for which it has room, and new higher relations of production never appear before the material conditions of their existence are matured in the womb of the old society.

That is the quotation I should like us to consider, Mr. Chairman.

CHAIRMAN: Thank you, Allen. Now, Streeter, you claim to be coming to the study of Marxism without any previous sytematic knowledge of it. Is there anything in that quotation which you would like Allen to clarify?

STREETER: There certainly is. I'm afraid I got little more than a vague general drift.

ALLEN: I think I may help you if I add a quotation from Engels.

STREETER: I don't know about that. It won't be like the other one will it? If so, I'd rather concentrate on one at a time.

ALLEN: No, it's not like that. It's an explanation, a more simple statement of what Marx says in the quotation I just gave. I think it will help.

CHAIRMAN: Very well then, let's have it. Where does Engels say it?

ALLEN: It is part of Engels' speech at the grave of Marx. He was trying to sum up the achievements of Marx and he said this:

> Marx discovered the simple fact (heretofore hidden beneath ideological overgrowths) that human beings must have food, drink, clothing and shelter first of all, before they can interest themselves in politics, science, art, religion and the like. This implies that the production of the immediately requisite material means of subsistence, and therewith the existing phase of development of a nation or an epoch, constitute the foundation upon which the state institutions, the legal outlooks, the artistic and even the religious ideas are built up. It implies that these latter must be explained out of the former, whereas the former have usually been explained as issuing from the latter.

There, Mr. Chairman, Engels gives you Marx's great discovery in a nutshell.

STREETER: Is that all Marx said in that other passage you read to us?

ALLEN: No, it is certainly not all that he said but it is the bare bones of it.

STREETER: I see. I think I can understand Engels. Suppose we start with what Engels has to say and then see if we can get at Marx's meaning through him.

ALLEN: That suits me.

STREETER: Well, have I understood Engels correctly? He says that we can explain state institutions, legal outlooks, artistic and religious ideas and so forth by the way in which men produce their means of subsistence.

ALLEN: That is correct.

STREETER: And is that what Marx says also?

ALLEN: Yes, that is what Marx says, though he says much more. You will notice that both men use the same picture to bring home what they mean. Marx speaks of a 'foundation' and a 'superstructure' and Engels talks of a 'foundation' on which other things are built up.

SOUTH: It is not wise, from a Marxist point of view to push this 'foundation-superstructure' metaphor too far.

ALLEN: That is a matter that could be argued, but at least we can see what they are driving at. Here is the foundation, the economic structure of society, the mode of production. That is the foundation, that is primary because, as Engels says, 'human beings must have food, drink, clothing and shelter first of all . . .'

STREETER: I see that.

ALLEN: Once it is stated it is clear as crystal. But of course, the economic structure of society is not the only aspect of society. There is the state, there are political ideas, religious ideas, ideas about the law and so forth. These Marx regards as the superstructure, as something built on the foundation, on the economic structure. You find the tendency to explain how men produce their means of subsistence by referring to their ideas. Thinkers have regarded men's ideas as determining how they live. Marx denies that this is so. 'It is not the consciousness of men which determines their existence,' he says.

STREETER: He thinks it is the other way round?

ALLEN: Yes, 'it is their social existence which determines their consciousness.' Notice that he is talking about their social existence. He is not thinking about men as isolated individuals, he is thinking about human society.

STREETER: Do you mean that Marx makes a division between what men do on the one hand and their ideas on the other and that he says that what they do determines what they think, rather than the other way about?

ALLEN: Yes, he does say that, but don't forget that he also makes a distinction in what they do. Their activities are not merely economic, they are also, for example, political, and he points out that their economic activities determine their political activities. Hence the economic is the foundation, the political is part of the superstructure. Bear in mind all the time that Marx is talking about society, he is not talking about individual men. It is no answer to Marx's argument to point to this or that worker and to say 'He has the same ideas as this or that capitalist therefore how can you say that the economic determines the ideological, the system of ideas.' That is no answer to Marx. He was well aware that individuals can develop a great variety of ideas or of political activities despite a similar economic background. Individuals have their ideas shaped by all sorts of forces which play upon them. Nevertheless the workers as a class, the capitalists as a class develop different ideas, different political policies and you can't explain them ultimately except as arising from the economic structure of society and the place of these classes in it. So it is with any aspect of social life. To explain it you must come back to the economic because it is the economic structure of society which determines it and upon which it rests.

STREETER: Do you mean to tell me that ideas have not played a great part in history? Aren't there cases where ideas have been put forward and where they have changed all sorts of social institutions including economic institutions themselves? What about the ideas of Christianity, for example, or, if you want to come further down in history, what about those men who believed it was wrong that such an institution as slavery should exist? Didn't they put forward their ideas, spread them, win support for them and didn't these ideas eventually help to overthrow slavery? Notice that I'm not overstating my case. I'm not saying that the ideas alone overthrew slavery. I am saying merely that they helped, or perhaps I should put it more strongly and say that they played an important part. All that seems to me to be obviously true. How can you answer that from a Marxist position?

ALLEN: I don't think there is any difficulty there for Marxism. Certainly Marx does not deny that ideas play an important part in history. What he does is to push the analysis further. He asks—'Whence do these ideas come and why is it that at one period of history they are not taken up and have on influence, whereas at another period they spread like a bushfire and have a tremendous social influence?'

Naturally I can't give a concrete analysis of the causes of any system of ideas that may have arisen in history. In order to give such an analysis we'd have to look very closely into the circumstances surrounding the origin of the system of ideas. In most cases I couldn't do it and even if I could there wouldn't be time to expound it.

STREETER: I understand that but nevertheless you will admit that ideas have arisen which have been opposed to the economic structure of the day. For example you find socialist ideas in the period of the rise and even in the period of the flourishing of capitalism.

ALLEN: Marxism not only admits that, it emphasises it. Don't forget that for Marx, the economic structure of society is not a simple thing. Don't forget the dialectic. There are contradictory features in the economic structure of society. And contradictions in ideologies arise out of these basic contradictions, out of the contradictions in the economic foundation. Take your own example. Is it so surprising that you find socialist ideas at the time when capitalism was rising or at the time when capitalism was flourishing? In the economic structure which we describe as capitalism there is the working class. Capitalism calls the working class into existence. Is it not perfectly compatible with the Marxist theory of history—I will say more than that—is it not demanded by the Marxist theory of history that as capitalism rises and flourishes we should find not only ideologies arising out of and supporting capitalism itself, but also ideologies opposed to it, arising out of and supporting the class exploited by capitalism? Is that not a fact?

STREETER: Yes, I'll have to admit that that fits in with the Marxist theory so far as I have understood it.

ALLEN: And so do your examples of Christianity and anti-slavery. Here we are concerned more with the conditions under which ideas catch on and become historical forces. I can say a great deal about that.

CHAIRMAN: Just a moment, Allen. I know that this matter of ideologies is relevant to the Marxist theory of history, but on the one hand it is only one branch of it and on the other hand we are going to devote a special discussion to it later on. So I'll ask you not to try to expound at length but simply to sketch the outlines of your answer. After all if members of groups are especially interested in this aspect there is nothing to prevent them discussing it at length now and seeing what you have to say about it later. So would you mind being brief?

ALLEN: Very well, Mr. Chairman. I must confess I warm to this subject because so many mistaken criticisms of

Marxism arise out of it. Nevertheless I realise we have to cover other points so here, in brief, is my answer: a system of ideas catches on if the economic structure or an aspect of the economic structure demands it, and the economic structure will change systems of ideas out of all recognition in order to make them suit its requirements. I hardly need seek a better example than the one with which Streeter supplied me, namely Christianity. Look through the history of Christianity and see if it isn't really different systems of ideas at different periods of history, of course all called 'Christianity' but in reality each an ideology suited to the economic structure of its day. As to 'anti-slavery' do you find this catching on and becoming a historical force before capitalism came along with its need for free labour, i.e. labour that it could hire and fire. Each of Streeter's examples supports the Marxist case as indeed any genuine historical examples must, since Marxism is the only scientific theory of history. I could say much more but I'll let it go at that for the present.

CHAIRMAN: Thank you, Allen. We must not forget that South has yet to make his criticisms. Have you anything more to raise Streeter?

STREETER: Yes, Mr. Chairman. I didn't grasp something Marx said about productive forces and productive relations. I'm wondering if Allen can tell us about that.

ALLEN: Yes, I'll be glad. So far we've only considered the broad picture—the economic foundation on the one hand and the superstructure on the other comprising things like politics, law, ideology and so on. But we can look more closely into either of these two main divisions and Marx does look more closely. In the passage I quoted he makes an important distinction within the economic. He speaks of 'material productive forces' on the one hand and of 'production relations' on the other hand. By material productive forces he means things like tools, machines, railways, ships and so on. By production relations he means the relations into which men enter in production such as employer and employee, buyer and seller, lord and serf and so on.

STREETER: I understand that now. According to the passage you quoted he thinks the two have inter-actions which are important for history?

ALLEN: That is correct. If you take a particular time in history, then the productive forces will have reached a certain stage of development and the production relations will be at a certain stage. But there is a rigidity about the production relations. They don't change easily. That is because there are exploiting classes resisting changes which will do away with the basis of their exploitation.

CHAIRMAN: I presume you do not need to go into that in detail now. You'll have an opportunity later when we talk about the class struggle.

ALLEN: Very well. All that I want to insist upon is that there is rigidity in the production relations. On the other hand the productive forces develop and as it were, press against the relations. The relations become fetters upon the forces. Consider, for example, how the relations prevailing under feudalism held up the development of means of transport and communication. Every local magnate had the right to levy tolls, make his own vexatious regulations and so on. Social organization on the economic side made it impossible for the means of transport and communication (which are an important part of production) to be developed—made it impossible, that is, unless the social organization on the economic side was changed. And that is what happens. As the productive forces develop they find the existing social relations in production more and more fetters upon them. Social tension mounts. Finally there is social revolution. A new set of production relations is born. There is a new economic structure of society, a new foundation—and this in turn transforms the superstructure.

STREETER: So that you could really say that within the economic structure the productive forces are basic, they determine the changes in the relations into which men enter in production and this determines the rest of social life.

ALLEN: That is so. That is the dialectic of history.

CHAIRMAN: We must not try to go further than that. We must be fair to South. He has yet to make his criticisms.

SOUTH: Well, Mr. Chairman, a great deal has been said and I can't very well traverse all of it but as you have pointed out, some of these issues will arise again and perhaps I shall have an opportunity to say more then. Before I attack the Marxist theory of history I would like to point out that there are valuable things in it. For instance I think Marx performed a valuable service in his stress on the role of the economic in history. The economic structure of society or, as I should prefer to say, the economic structures do have their influence upon politics, upon religion, upon law, upon ideas. It is true that it tended to be overlooked, that there was a tendency to talk as if ideas alone made history or as if political activity made history and so on. Marx provided a healthy corrective to all that. There is another important point about Marx's theory too and I must confess to some surprise that nobody has mentioned it, though it was stated right at the beginning of the quotation which Allen read out to us and it was implicit right through that quotation.

STREETER: What is this important point South?

SOUTH: You remember Marx says '. . . men enter into determined and necessary relations with each other which are independent of their wills . . .' Notice that 'determined relations . . . independent of their wills'. Throughout Marx's thought there runs this strand of historical determinism, i.e. the theory that there are laws in history, that historical forces operate in regular ways and that men are caught up in them and as social beings are moulded by history, and that they don't stand, as it were, outside of history and mould it. I am not saying that Marx is always consistent on this point but he does make it and, in my opinion, there can be no scientific study of history or politics or economics, or other social phenomena without it.

CHAIRMAN: We'll note this point that you've made South, but I want to remind you that you are helping us to probe Marxism from the point of view of one who is opposed to it. If you don't come round to your opposition soon we'll have nothing at all said against the Marxist theory of history and I'm sure there must be arguments against it which would be worthwhile to consider.

SOUTH: There are plenty Mr. Chairman. Nevertheless I must remind you that this is a discussion not a debate. In a discussion one's primary responsibility is to the truth, not to a 'side' and if there are important truths in the position to which one is opposed and if nobody has brought them out, then I think it is one's business to bring them out. A discussion is a co-operative effort to discover truths, not simply a battle, though there may be elements of a battle in it.

CHAIRMAN: Quite so. I admit I may have been hasty. Nevertheless time is getting on. Even as it is you will have to confine yourself to the briefest exposition of a few main points.

SOUTH: Well, Mr. Chairman, so long as we do not lose sight of the valuable truths in the Marxist theory of history I am content to go on to show where it is false. My main criticism of it is that it is Monist.

STREETER: It is what?

SOUTH: Monist—that is to say it reduces history to one thing, to one force whereas I say that there are many forces in history, that they interact and that you can't talk about any one of them as basic or as foundation or however else you like to put it. You remember I told you before that I was a pluralist, I believe there is a plurality of forces in anything, and society or history is no exception.

STREETER: But surely South, if we can take any notice of Allen at all, if he is not making it all up, Marx recognizes many forces. He talks about the economic structure. It is true he calls this the foundation but he doesn't deny that there are politics, law, religion and the rest.

SOUTH: Of course he doesn't deny them. What Monist could ever deny entirely that many forces exist, without reducing his position to obvious absurdity. Marx talks about them and often in his theories, especially when he is dealing with concrete historical questions, he allows them real historical power, that is, he talks about them as if they share in the making of history. He must do that when he comes to talk about concrete historical situations or he'd have nothing to say. That is because the pluralist position, the interactionist position is the true one.

STREETER: Well if he does allow that they are real historical forces, what is the point of your criticism?

SOUTH: The point of my criticism is that in his general theory he does not allow that they are real historical forces. He keeps a certain plausibility in his theory of history by shifting from one position to another. You consider the quotation

Allen gave us. What is Marx's position there? The economic structure determines everything. If it is changed the whole superstructure is changed. There is no suggestion that the superstructure changes the foundation. In fact in the realm of ideas Marx explicitly denies it. He is not content to say 'I admit that consciousness determines man's existence but don't forget that their existence also determines their consciousness'. That would be a pluralist position, that would admit interaction, that would be perfectly sound and a healthy corrective for those who believe that ideas or consciousness achieve everything, for those, that is, who fall into a historical monism in a different direction. Marx is not content with that. He leans right over the other way. He simply denies flat that consciousness determines existence. I believe that that is false. It is easy to exaggerate the part that our ideas play in determining what we do but it is one thing to correct that exaggeration, it is a different thing to deny that our ideas have any influence at all on what we do or are. And if Marx's statement does not mean that, then what does it mean? You will search in vain through that passage for an admission that the economic structure of society is shaped by the superstructural elements of society.

It is the same with Allen's examples. He can show quite rightly that anti-slavery ideas would not have had the effect they did without a certain economic structure of society. That is correct. I have no quarrel with that at all. What I am emphasizing is that it is equally true to say that the economic structure of society would not have had its effects without anti-slavery ideas. Each force, the ideological and the economic played its part, each affected the other. The same with politics, the same with law, the same with religion, the same with many other forces. It may be possible to show that the economic structure of society is a very important force, it may even be possible to show that in some sense it is the most important force. I say that may be possible. I am not going to argue whether it is or not. All that I am going to say is that it is certainly impossible to make history a one way street, to make the economic the sole determining factor, and that is what Marxism does.

ALLEN: Mr. Chairman, I really must interpose. I should

like to have remained silent but this is so gross a mis-representation that I feel I must speak. Fortunately we have something explicit on this point from Engels. This kind of criticism that we have heard from South was made in Engels' day, and he answered it for all time. I'd like to read the passage.

CHAIRMAN: I don't know that I can allow that since South has so little time, unless South himself wishes it.

SOUTH: By all means. I don't see how Engels can possibly get away from Marxist Monism, and it would be interesting to hear the passage in which Allen thinks that he does get away from it.

ALLEN: Very well. I will quote without comment. That should be sufficient. This is from a letter Engels wrote to Bloch in 1890:

According to the materialist conception of history, the production and reproduction of real life constitutes *in the last instance* the determining factor of history. Neither Marx nor I ever maintained more. Now when someone comes along and distorts this to mean that the economic factor is the *sole* determining factor, he is converting the former proposition into a meaning-less, abstract and absurd phrase. The economic situation is the basis but the various factors of the superstructure—the political forms of the class struggle and its results—constitutions, etc. established by victorious classes after hard-won battles—legal forms and even the reflexes of all these real struggles in the brain of the participants, political, jural, philosophical theories, religious conceptions and their further development into systema-tic dogmas—all these exercise an influence upon the course of historical struggles, and in many cases determine for the most part their *form*. There is a reciprocity between all these factors in which, finally, through the endless array of contingencies . . . the economic movement asserts itself as necessary . . . We ourselves make our own history, but, first of all, under very definite presuppositions and conditions. Among these are the economic which are finally decisive. But there are also the political, etc. Yes, even the ghostly traditions which haunt the minds of men play a role albeit not a decisive one.

STREETER: You had me half convinced, South, but that settles it. There's no doubt about it now. Engels gives a big list of factors which he recognizes and he also says explicitly 'There is a reciprocity between all these factors . . .' What more could you want than that? If that is not pluralism and interactionism I don't know what is. You must give up your criticism now.

SOUTH: On the contrary that passage from Engels confirms my criticism up to the hilt. Did you ever come across a passage where a man was more obviously wriggling desperately to hold on to one thing while pretending to admit something else which is incompatible with it? Engels sees quite clearly that to say that 'the economic factor is the *sole* determining factor' is absurd. It is impossible to stand on that position. He must give it up. He must admit a plurality of forces and their role. But if he does, nothing is left of the distinctively Marxist conception of history. All he can do is to jump desperately from one position to the other.

Notice how every time he gives something away he takes it back again. The economic is not the sole determining factor (he's given it away) . . . but in the last instance it is the determining factor (he's taken it back). There is a reciprocity between all these factors (he's given it away) . . . but finally the economic asserts itself as necessary (he's taken it back). Among the conditions under which we make our history are the economic (he's given it away) . . . but the economic are finally decisive (he's taken it back). Even the ghostly traditions play a role (he's given it away) . . . but not a decisive one (he's taken it back).

This is not serious theorizing. It is simply an apologist trying to defend an untenable theory from sound criticism by verbal slickness. But it won't do. If 'in the last instance' the economic is 'the determining factor of history' then what is left for any other factor to determine? If other factors play their part then how can the economic be *the* determining factor in the last instance or any other instance? If the economic is 'decisive' then this means *it* decides what happens and if other factors are 'not decisive' then this means that they don't decide what happens. In that case there is no role for them to play. Engels tells us that finally the economic movement asserts itself as necessary. But what does he mean by that? By 'finally' he cannot mean that the economic is the final determinant of every event because that would be treating it straight out as the sole determining factor. If he means that there is an elapse of time in which the economic does not get its way but finally (i.e. in the long run) it does, then he is simply saying that part of the time the economic gets its way and part of the time other

things get their way. That certainly gives no basis for assign-
ing a special role to the economic, especially when we
remember that there is no 'finality' in history, no 'last
instance', but only a continuing complexity.

Surely I don't need to say much more. The reference to
other factors determining the *form* of historical struggles does
not help Engels at all. It is a word of vague meaning. Presum-
ably he means to contrast it with 'substance'. Just what the
distinction would be is difficult if not impossible to specify.
But suppose we waive that point, suppose we assume there is a
distinction between the form and the substance of historical
struggles. The question then arises—does the form influence
the substance? If it does then the other factors influence the
substance (through their influence on the 'form'), and are in no
different position from the economic. If it does not then
Engels is reserving for the economic, the role of the sole
determining factor of the substance of history. He is abandon-
ing genuine pluralism and interactionism. The trouble is, he is
trying to reconcile the irreconcilable.

Well, Mr. Chairman, my main point is that the Marxist
theory of history is a monist doctrine, it allows only one factor
in history. That is the position as Marx stated it. Such a
doctrine is impossible to maintain. It cannot cope with
explaining concrete historical situations. Consequently it is
necessary to abandon it in answering criticisms or explaining
historical situations, and appearances can be kept up only by
skipping from that theory to another which contradicts it.

CHAIRMAN: Thank you South. I take it we all realize that
there are other aspects of the Marxist theory of history which
will come up in later discussions. We have simply concen-
trated on the central points of it.

III

The Class Struggle

CHAIRMAN: Last time we met we discussed the Marxist theory of history, in particular the connection between what the Marxists call the economic base and what they call the superstructure, that is between the material forces of production and the relations of men in production on the one hand and, on the other hand, their religion, their legal theory, their politics, their ideology and so on. But we admitted that there were other aspects of the Marxist theory of history.

STREETER: Yes, there is one thing that puzzles me about all this. We were talking about the Marxist theory of history, and we gave no serious attention to 'classes'. I admit I don't know much about Marxism and maybe I'm wrong but I have been under the impression that Marxism is a theory about class struggles. All that business about foundation and superstructure was news to me. Surely the Marxists have something to say about classes—the working class and the capitalists and so on. If they do, how do they fit it in with this other theory about the economic basis and the superstructure of society?

CHAIRMAN: Well, Allen can tell us about that.

ALLEN: There is no special difficulty about it. The theory that we discussed at our last meeting is undoubtedly the Marxist theory of history. But there is no contradiction between that and the class theory of history. The class theory of history fits in to the materialist conception of history. Indeed it completes it and is required by it.

STREETER: You may be right but I can't see it. You'll have to explain it in more detail.

ALLEN: It is easily enough explained. There are material forces of production (tools, machines, and so on) but it is men who make them or find them and use them. There are relations in production but it is men who enter into these relations. This man is an employer, that man is an employee. There are ideologies, but it is men who believe them. There are political struggles but it is men who fight them.

STREETER: You mean that we don't have to think of these things as abstractions.

ALLEN: Exactly. That is precisely what Marxism maintains. History is made by men, real living men. Men produce, men enter into relations in production, men struggle politically, men believe ideologies. What Marx and Engels show is the way in which the activities of men affect one another, the way their production which is basic, affects their politics and their ideologies and all the rest of it.

STREETER: I think I understand that, but I can't see what it has to do with classes or the class struggle.

ALLEN: The connection is simple enough. Men are not isolated individuals. They are social beings. They enter into relations in the process of production. This one owns the means of production (say a factory), that one does not own the means of production. All that he is in a position to contribute to the process of production is his labour. So he sells his labour in order to keep alive. The first man here is a capitalist. He supplies capital. The second is a worker.

STREETER: And there are many capitalists and many workers and so you have a class of capitalists and a class of workers.

ALLEN: That is correct as far as it goes but it is not the whole story. A class is not simply a total of individuals. These individuals are organized in various ways in the process of production and this is part of the characteristics of the class too.

STREETER: You mean that we find joint stock companies, banks with money on loan to industry as well as teams of workers and division of labour by trades and that sort of thing?

ALLEN: Yes, I mean that. Those are characteristics on the one hand of the capitalist class and on the other hand of the working class. But you must not forget either that there are bodies like Chambers of Manufacturers and trades unions and political parties in which classes find expression.

STREETER: I see. And are the workers and the capitalists the only two classes?

ALLEN: No, of course not. Anyone who thought that would miss the whole point of the class theory as a theory of history. Workers and capitalists as classes emerge at only a late stage in history. According to Marx and Engels there is a primitive classless phase of society, a phase before private property, a phase of primitive communism. We find that classes emerge with the emergence of private property in the means of production. We find those who own this property and those who don't. There are three main phases of history—the phase of slave society where you find slave-owners and slaves, the feudal phase where you find feudal lords and serfs, and the capitalist phase where you find capitalists and workers.

STREETER: Surely Allen, if Marx and Engels say that, they are over-simplifying their account of history. After all, you have only to look about you to find people in our society that you can't classify as either capitalists or workers.

ALLEN: You forget, Streeter, that I was telling you only the main phases and the main classes. Marx and Engels were not at all simple minded in this theory. They allowed for all kinds of complications. They knew that these phases overlapped, for example, that you could find slavery persisting into feudal and even into capitalist society and they knew as well that there were various intermediate classes. For example in any kind of class society you may find men who own and work their own land. In some capitalist countries these peasants constitute the bulk of what Marx calls the petty-bourgeoisie, a class which includes also working owners in small industrial concerns and shops. In feudal society there are the guildsmen of the towns, themselves divided into various layers. There are all sorts of complications. I haven't time to go into them now. If you want to look into them more closely you can read Bukharin's *Historical Materialism*.

STREETER: I will, but for the present, what about this difficulty—a worker may save his earnings and invest them. Or he might receive a small inheritance or win a lottery and invest. He still goes on working for wages. What are you going to say about him?

ALLEN: That is an easy one. It simply means that he is a member of both classes. These people are very interesting at a time when the class struggle becomes acute. They and the petty bourgeoisie in general find themselves pulled both ways between the two main clashing classes. They waver. In many cases their support for one side or the other is decisive for the issue of the particular struggle.

STREETER: I see. And the Marxist theory is that we have a struggle between the class that owns the means of production and the class that does not?

ALLEN: That is part of the theory but it is far from the whole of it. We also find struggles between classes based on different forms of ownership. For example the capitalists fought against and overthrew the feudal lords, substituting capitalism for feudalism. It is not a simple process. It may last for a very long time and the struggle takes on many forms such as direct economic competition, struggles for different political forms such as a monarchy versus a parliament, ideological forms—such as a new form of religious belief replacing an old form. These struggles last a long time, at different stages involve open violence and, of course, at all times involve a certain amount of violence in maintaining the existing state against its opponents.

STREETER: So Marx and Engels advocate violence in these class struggles?

ALLEN: It is not a case of advocating violence. It is a matter of describing what happens. You look at the struggle between feudalism and capitalism and you will see that a certain amount of violence was involved all the time; and at special periods, when the very foundations were at stake there was a great deal of violence. The clash took on an especially clear cut character.

STREETER: You mean in the French Revolution for example.

ALLEN: Yes, that is one example. The so-called Puritan revolution in England is another openly violent phase of the same struggle.

STREETER: I see. And all this you say is linked up with the Marxist idea of changes in the relationships in production.

ALLEN: These are the changes in production relations. You remember that Marx says that the existing production relations become fetters upon the forces of production. You could say that in another way namely that the existing ruling class with the rights, privileges and systems of ideas it has established is an obstruction to the development of the means of production. Consider how a feudal system with its local regulations, its local magnates' rights over tolls, land and so on would hamper the development of railways, roads and indeed of the requirements of widespread trade in general. In order to develop the forces of production it was necessary to overthrow the feudal class. There are other aspects too. At a certain stage it is necessary to have workers you can hire and fire. Neither slaves nor serfs fit in to that category. Hence it was necessary to get rid of the systems which involved these classes.

STREETER: And it is another class which does this abolishing? It was the capitalists who abolished feudalism?

ALLEN: In certain countries, yes. In other countries which developed later you may find a different pattern of development. The workers may be so strong before the capitalists make their revolution that the capitalists are afraid to move lest they jeopardize the whole system of property relationships. In that case, the workers may take the lead in overthrowing feudalism or its remnants. However that introduces a complication which we may be wiser not to enter upon now.

STREETER: I'm glad you're not going to go into the details of that. I think I get its general drift—but I'm bothered about another problem. In our last discussion you said, and you quoted Marx to support you, that it was the forces of production which changed the production relations or, according to the way you are talking now, it was the forces of production which overthrew old classes. That seemed queer to me at the time; I mean it sounds as if railway engines go around shooting up feudal lords or something of that kind. What you are saying now seems to me to make more sense—the capitalists eliminate the feudal lords. I can understand that but the other seems to me to be nonsense. Which is Marx's position?

ALLEN: Both. There is no inconsistency between them. Of course men make their own history. Marx leaves no doubt about that. The capitalists fight and overthrow feudalism. But why do they fight and why are they able to win?

STREETER: Because they are more up to date in their methods I suppose.

ALLEN: That is exactly it. They stand for the developing forces of production. They stand for a system which can develop those forces of production further—I am speaking of a past period of history, of course. New forces of production have been developing within feudalism. Along with them have developed new classes. The new society is there in embryo in the old. From being an insignificant force it grows to a mighty opposition. The machines themselves press in the direction of social change. They require a different kind of social organization of production. Small machines worked by hand, for example, can be housed and operated in the cottage of a peasant or a town artisan. But when you get large power driven machinery with other heavy machinery required to generate the power you have to have factories, which means you have to have large amounts of capital and a labour force. The developments in the material forces of production themselves bring about changes in the relationships in production, in other words call into being new classes. And when these new classes fight the old ruling classes they are fighting not only on behalf of privileges and rights for themselves, they are fighting also on behalf of the developing material forces of production, forces which can be developed within *their* system but which are hampered by the old system. You might say that the material forces are expressed in or fight through the rising or revolutionary class. So the two theories are not really distinct. They are different aspects of the same theory. A revolutionary class fights on behalf of a new system of production which itself involves developing material productive forces.

STREETER: I must admit that's remarkable. I see the argument. I think there's something in that. There is no doubt that Marx has thought it all out. But there's still a point I would like cleared up. I suppose he has thought out this too. All the same I will state my objection. These revolutions are supposed to be about systems of production. You say that the revolutionary class is fighting for one system of production against another. That might be true about the Russian revolution but it has always seemed to me that revolutions have something to do with changing the State. After all the English Puritans chopped off the head of Charles I, the French revolutionaries did the same to Louis XVI. Even the Russians changed their state. If you leave out the Russians, the other don't seem to have talked so much about the system of production as about the proper form of state, about tyranny, about liberty, equality, and fraternity and all the rest of it. What has Marx to say to that?

CHAIRMAN: Before you answer that Allen, I want to remind you that these points will be raised in later discussions. So will you now confine yourself to the bare essentials just sufficiently to round out the theory. We can handle the problems in detail later.

ALLEN: Very well, Mr. Chairman. I will cover these and other points briefly. The Marxist theory is this: a ruling class has its own state. The revolutionary overthrow of that class means the overthrow of its state and the substitution of a new state. That is the form taken by the political side of a struggle which is basically economic. Also a ruling class has its appropriate ideology which at its peak dominates large sections of society. Part of the process of the decline of a ruling class consists in the decline in the acceptance of its ideology. A new class, a revolutionary class also has its ideology, its system of ideas in the name of which it fights. This ideology does not describe exactly what is happening. Men in history are largely ignorant of what they are doing and describe it in mistaken terms. They say they are fighting for liberty and in fact are fighting for the liberty of private capital. That is the sort of thing.

I might say more about the difference between the workers as a revolutionary class and all previous revolutionary classes but I may be wiser Mr. Chairman to leave that until a later discussion. For the present I will content myself with saying this: all previous revolutionary classes have been minorities and propertied and therefore exploiting, whereas the working class is a majority, propertyless and therefore not exploiting. That is why all previous revolutions, whatever advances they involved, have perpetuated exploitation even if in new forms whereas the working class or proletarian revolution will end exploitation and class division, will end the phase of history as the story of the class struggle and will begin truly human history.

CHAIRMAN: Thank you, Allen. I'll ask South not to criticize yet the latter part of what you had to say. We'll save that up for later discussions. Taking the main points of Allen's case, South, are you going to accept all that or criticize all of it or what?

SOUTH: I am going to accept some of it, Mr. Chairman, but not all of it. It seems to me to be a gross oversimplification.

STREETER: That is what I was inclined to think but it seems that Marx has allowed for more complications than I realized.

SOUTH: No doubt, but he has nevertheless grossly over-simplified.

STREETER: How?

SOUTH: Just a moment. Let me first of all say what I accept in the Marxist theory.

First I admit that there are slave owners and slaves, feudal lords and serfs, capitalists and workers, landlords, petty bourgeoisie and so on. Men do enter into certain relations in production and their position there does influence their out-look, their politics and the rest of their social life. My pluralist theory leads me to admit that. It also leads me to admit that you do find struggles between classes. I further admit that rulers existing at any given time can hold up the development of productive forces.

STREETER: Just a moment, South. You said rulers there. Allen would certainly have said ruling class. Is there any significance in that or was it just your way of talking?

SOUTH: It *is* my way of talking, but it is significant that that is my way of talking. I do not believe it is correct to speak of the ruling class if we use 'class' in the Marxist sense.

STREETER: I think you had better explain a bit more. I don't follow.

SOUTH: Wait a moment. Let me go back a bit. You remember that I told you in our last discussion that the Marx-ist theory of history was monist, that it recognized only one force in history namely the economic, in spite of Engels' attempts to maintain this position and at the same time to accept pluralism—an attempt which makes use of verbal dex-terity alone. Well here we have another example of that monism. History is a very complex thing. We find literary movements rising and falling, religions changing in doctrine and organizational form, different philosophical systems being worked out—and I might add certain main lines of development running through them, we find monarchies, republics, parliaments, oligarchies, dictators, peace and war between different forces and with changing alliances, we find the development of legal traditions and their variations, the arts taking on various forms and so on. We are asked to believe that all these things can be explained in terms of the struggle between different classes engaged in material production. I don't believe it.

STREETER: You don't believe it but that is not an argument. I didn't believe it either but Allen has convinced me. He showed us that this class struggle is more complex and has more far-reaching effects than we thought.

SOUTH: Than you thought. But does it not strike you as strange that this class theory of history has not been widely accepted amongst those making a detailed study of history? Some have accepted it, of course, but I suggest that all they can show is that there is a struggle between classes and that this has an influence on other spheres of social life. They can show that and it is only what we expect if we accept the position that the different social forces interact. But they can't show more than that and they have to show more than that if the class theory is to stand up.

STREETER: Can you give us an example?

SOUTH: I can give you plenty. Here is one. In the nineteenth century Russia was in many ways a backward country. It was only in 1861 that serfdom was abolished. Illiteracy was widespread. Technologically the country was backward. Yet out of this backward country came a magnificent literature. Men like Dostoevsky and Tolstoy produced great novels, novels showing a remarkable penetration into human psychology and sense of artistry. No doubt someone studying these writers could point to the influence of class relations on these writers and their books but I venture to suggest this—it would be a very incomplete account you could give of them on that basis. One other important factor that you'd have to take into account would be the tradition of literature. The same goes for the literature of Shakespearian England. You can show the *influence* of class but you can't explain it all in class terms, and the part you can't explain in that way is also part of history.

STREETER: I see that but what about politics?

SOUTH: Politics is no different. It is simply not true that classes act as political units. Of course Marx admits that sections of a class, even a class as a whole has temporary aberrations from the path of its true interests. Nevertheless he says it has a solidarity of interests which prevails in the long run. I deny that. There are other forces besides classes and they cut across class lines.

STREETER: Can you give us some examples?

SOUTH: They exist in plenty. You take Roman Catholicism. You may explain its rise in class terms if you wish. I will not bother now to go into the question of its origin because I don't need to do that for my argument. However it originated there it has been for a very long time. It has persisted through various systems of class relations. It is a force in itself and those who are part of it have been drawn from various classes. It constitutes a basis of division in the capitalist class and in the working class. I mean you have Catholic and non-Catholic capitalists, workers, peasants and so on.

STREETER: But I understood that the Marxists had given an explanation of Catholicism as an ideology favourable to the exploiting class.

SOUTH: They give an explanation of all religion as ideology favourable to exploiting classes. But even if that is true it is not good enough to establish a class theory of history. What they have to show is that Roman Catholicism or the various branches of Protestantism or Islam or whatever it is, has no history of its own but is simply an expression of class struggle. Even if Roman Catholicism is an ideology of the ruling class, they have to explain why it has suited several different ruling classes, why part of one ruling class adopts it while another part adopts Protestantism and another part atheism. You can make these broad generalizations as the Marxists do but you can sustain them only by ignoring variations, only by assuming when you have shown that the class struggle influences a thing like the religious outlook in a given community, that you have shown that it explains it entirely. These are quite different things.

And then, of course, you can approach the matter from the other side.

STREETER: What do you mean by 'from the other side'?

SOUTH: You can show that a force like the religious outlook influences the development of classes. Take Spain under the early Hapsburg kings. They drove out the Moors and the Jews thereby contributing towards the weakening of rising capitalism there. Don't you agree that religion played an important role in that?

STREETER: Maybe it did, but weren't there other factors? For example didn't the importation of gold from the new world lead to inflation and cripple Spain's export trade?

SOUTH: Of course there were other factors. That is what I am arguing all the time. The process is complex and it is unsound to try to boil it all down to one factor—the economic or any other. It is unsound to try to boil all social struggles down to one struggle—the class struggle or any other. We find struggles between different forces of various kinds. A war between nations, for example, is not a class struggle but it is a part of history. On each side you sometimes find capitalists, workers, petty bourgeoisie and so on. Even if the war happens to be about economic issues the lines of division are not lines between classes, they are lines between nations.

STREETER: That looks like a bull's eye to me.

SOUTH: No more than any of the other points I have made.

STREETER: Well, suppose we do reject class struggle as what history is, can you substitute anything else?

SOUTH: If you tried to substitute any single thing you would be missing the point of my criticism. Marxism is trying to reduce all social conflict to conflict between economic classes. I am denying this. But I am denying more than this. I am denying that you can reduce it to one kind of conflict at all.

STREETER: You are really saying that there is economic conflict but there is also religious conflict, moral conflict, political conflict, legal conflict . . .

SOUTH: Conflict between science and obscurantism, conflict between sexual customs, conflict between nations, between states and so on.

STREETER: Wait a moment. A point has just struck me. The Marxists talk about class struggle; we've been talking about all sorts of conflicts. But is there nothing in history apart from struggles and conflicts? Surely there is co-operation too.

SOUTH: I quite agree. The Marxist position is better stated as History is the story of class relations. And the pluralist position might be put that history is the story of relations between a plurality of social forces, including economic classes but including many others as well.

CHAIRMAN: Our time is running out, South. Do you want to contest that a ruling class can become a fetter upon the material means of production and that a revolutionary class can ensure their further development?

SOUTH: In a sense I want to deny that. I deny that the rulers ever are simply an economic class. We can speak of an economic class as dominant in production and as wielding power in the state but that is only loose speaking and is never the whole story. Mixed in with the economic class may be various other forces. For example a church may be very powerful and by its ideas have partly captured the leading economic class itself, so that it places limitations upon its pursuit of its purely economic objectives. We may find certain powerful political traditions, powerful ideological traditions in general. Science may be held in high esteem or perhaps literature, or various forms of art. All these things can enter into the rulers and, if they do, then rightly understood this mixture of forces is the ruler. Even the dictator is under the sway of sets of ideas, of certain ways of acting. These are the rulers.

STREETER: But can they fetter the material forces of production and can new ones coming to the top in a revolution, develop those forces?

SOUTH: Of course that can happen, but notice that my position here differs from the Marxist. According to Marxism a revolution is part of the path upwards. They have their conception of counter-revolution to indicate a step backwards. But that very way of putting it suggests a direction in history, a direction which is progress. I deny this. I assert instead that sometimes you have progress, sometimes you have retrogression. The very thing which is called a revolution may be an overturning of one social set-up and the substitution of a new one yet that new one may involve a decline in all the major social spheres, a decline eventually into barbarism. That can happen. Look at Rome.

IV

The State

CHAIRMAN: I thought that, in our fourth discussion, we might look at the Marxist theory of the state. As usual Allen here will present the Marxist view, South will present the criticism of it . . .

SOUTH: From a pluralist point of view.

CHAIRMAN: Yes, from a pluralist point of view. And Streeter will ask such questions or make such criticisms as occur to him as a man with no expert knowledge of Marxism. Does it suit each of you to consider the state now?

STREETER: It makes no difference to me.

SOUTH: I'm satisfied. The theory of the state certainly has close links with what we have already discussed.

ALLEN: I think it follows on very well from the theory of class struggle. Indeed that theory would not be complete without it.

CHAIRMAN: Good, then it seems that we are all agreed it is proper to consider the Marxist theory of the state at this stage. I think we might follow our usual procedure and let Allen begin with an exposition of the Marxist position.

ALLEN: I will mention first, Mr. Chairman, a few books which might be helpful. There is Friedrich Engels's book *The Origin of the Family, Private Property, and the State.* Then there is the unfinished book by V. I. Lenin *State and Revolution.* It is maintained by some Marxists that Lenin's work is not orthodox Marxism on all points.

STREETER: Who says that?

ALLEN: I was just coming to that point. I think as good a criticism as any is to be found in Lucien Laurat's work *Marxism and Democracy.*

STREETER: You will be telling us where these differences of opinion arise later on, I suppose.

ALLEN: No, I don't think I will. Not tonight at any rate. They mainly concern points we shall be discussing when we come to talk about the Dictatorship of the Proletariat. I shall concentrate tonight on points of agreement.

STREETER: You mean points of agreement among Marxists.

ALLEN: Yes, among Marxists.

CHAIRMAN: You said, Allen, that the Marxists' theory of the state has close links with what we have already discussed, with the theory of class struggle . . .

ALLEN: Yes, with the theory of class struggle and with the theory of history. Marxism is a system. It fits together. It is not a collection of disconnected doctrines.

CHAIRMAN: I understand that. Could you make a beginning then by telling us how the theory of the state connects with these other theories?

ALLEN: I was going to do that. You remember how, in his theory of history, Marx regarded the economic structure of society as the basis or foundation and other aspects of social life as the superstructure resting upon that foundation, changing as it changes.

STREETER: Yes, I remember that. So for Marxism the State is part of the superstructure and its nature will be determined by the economic foundation of society?

ALLEN: Exactly. But Marxism does not leave the matter in that general form; it gives a more precise account of the state.

STREETER: Through the theory of classes?

ALLEN: Yes. You remember that the economic structure of society includes the relations into which men enter in production. These relations are class relations—feudal lords and serfs, bourgeoisie and proletariat . . .

STREETER: That is capitalists and workers.

ALLEN: Yes. It is only if you bear in mind the Marxist division of society into classes, or, more exactly, the fact that Marxism recognizes that society is divided into economic classes that you can understand the Marxist theory of the state. If you do bear in mind the fact of class struggle, the main outlines of the Marxist theory of the state are comparatively easy to grasp. I think the best way for me to state the theory is by means of quotations from Engels's *Origin of the Family, Private Property and the State.*

STREETER: I don't altogether favour these quotations. They're nearly always too difficult.

ALLEN: I don't see how you can master Marxism if you're not prepared to wrestle with what Marx and Engels said. In any case I don't think these are particularly difficult. Here is the first.

STREETER: From Engels?

ALLEN: From Engels:

The state is by no means a power imposed on society from the outside. . . . Rather, it is a product of society at a certain stage of development; it is the admission that this society has become entangled in an insoluble contradiction with itself, that it is cleft into irreconcilable antagonisms which it is powerless to dispel. But in order that these antagonisms, classes with conflicting economic interests, may not consume themselves and society in sterile struggle, a power apparently standing above society becomes necessary, whose purpose is to moderate the conflict and keep it within the bounds of 'order'; and this power arising out of society, but placing itself above it, and increasingly separating itself from it, is the state.

Is that clear enough?

STREETER: I understand the general drift. Could I have a look at it?

ALLEN: Certainly.

STREETER: I agree with Engels that the state is not imposed on society from the outside. I suppose we can leave out of account cases of conquest by an outside state which thus imposes itself because that outside state first had to arise from a society.

ALLEN: There are other considerations too.

STREETER: Maybe. Anyway I don't want to make an issue of those cases so we'll leave them on one side. The main point is that states are a product of society. I think I agree with that.

ALLEN: But notice that he says that the state 'is a product of society *at a certain stage of development*'.

STREETER: I was just considering that. Does he mean that there are societies without states?

ALLEN: There are or were. He argues that the state arises

where private property in the means of production and hence economic classes arise. It is the product of conflict of classes.

STREETER: I see. So he must hold that there are or were societies without private property in the means of production and without classes.

ALLEN: He does. This is set out in his book. He bases it on independent anthropological evidence too.

STREETER: I'm afraid I'll just have to take his word about that or rather keep an open mind. I don't know the facts or the evidence. But the main thing for us to consider is this: where the state exists, can it be explained in the Marxist way?

CHAIRMAN: Quite so.

STREETER: Well I have a question about that. Engels says that where you have class conflict in order to avoid sterile struggle 'a power apparently standing above society becomes necessary, whose purpose is to moderate the conflict and keep it within the bounds of "order".' Now my question is: where does this power—this state—come from? Engels says it arises out of society. From where in society?

ALLEN: I don't see any special difficulty there.

STREETER: Let me see if I can explain my difficulty. I know that Marx and Engels think that there are several classes in society, but suppose that to simplify matters we say there are only two—say capitalists and workers.

ALLEN: Very well. I'll grant that for the sake of argument.

STREETER: Then according to the Marxist position capitalists struggle against workers, workers against capitalists. Each is trying to win.

ALLEN: That is correct.

STREETER: Then who wants to moderate the struggle, who wants to keep it within the bounds of order?

ALLEN: Now I see your difficulty. I think I can answer best by another quotation from Engels:

As the state arose out of the need to hold class antagonisms in check, but as it, at the same time, arose in the midst of the conflict of those classes, it is, as a rule, the state of the most powerful, economically dominant class, which by virtue thereof becomes also the dominant class politically, and thus acquires new means of holding down and exploiting the oppressed class . . .

So the answer to your question in your own example would be: where the capitalists are the economically dominant class then the state comes from them, it is a capitalist state.

STREETER: But why should they want to moderate the class struggle to keep order? Surely they want to win it.

ALLEN: That is true, but if you hold the upper hand then to moderate the conflict is one way to continue holding the upper hand. You want to stabilize the position with yourself on top, in other words to keep 'order'. You don't want fights breaking out on every issue.

STREETER: I see. There are other points I don't quite understand. Engels puts *order* in inverted commas and you say it as if you do too. Why is that?

ALLEN: That is because there are different kinds of 'order'. One arrangement that suits the ruling class, it will call 'order'. Any conduct that fits in with that arrangement it will call 'orderly' conduct, and any conduct that clashes with that arrangement it will call disorderly conduct.

STREETER: Can you give me an example?

ALLEN: Plenty. Suppose you have an hereditary landed aristocracy which is the ruling class. Anything which suits the aristocracy it will call order. For example, aristocrats may have the right to hunt game over the land of their tenants. They will regard that as no breach of order. If the tenants organize to prevent it they will regard that as disorderly.

STREETER: I can see that but what about capitalists and workers?

ALLEN: Surely you get the same sort of thing there. If workers go on strike that is 'disorder'—'anarchy' and so on. Read your daily papers. But if an employer sacks a man, that is quite 'orderly'. The 'order' which a ruling class imposes is always its own 'order', the 'order' which suits it. From a capitalist point of view the pickets that by violence try to prevent strike breaking are 'disorderly', but the police or troops that by violence try to break up the pickets are not 'disorderly' but are supposed to be defending 'order'. It all depends on the point of view. They are defending capitalist order, they are attacking working class order.

STREETER: But surely police and troops are especially appointed by society to keep order. There is a difference between their legal action and the illegal action of say strike pickets.

ALLEN: What difference is there except that they are defending one kind of order and not another, and that their masters have been strong enough to get their 'order' established and recognized in laws? Don't forget that the laws are themselves a product of the class struggle and that the ruling class is able to establish laws which suit it, in particular which defend its property system. On this question of a police force, troops and so on, Engels has this to say: a distinguishing characteristic of the state 'is the establishment of a *public force*, which is no longer absolutely identical with the population organizing itself as an armed power. This special public force is necessary, because a self-acting armed organization of the population has become impossible since the cleavage of society into classes. . . . This public force exists in every state; it consists not merely of armed men, but of material appendages, prisons and repressive institutions of all kinds, of which genteel society knew nothing . . .'

STREETER: He means that you get only a section of the population armed?

ALLEN: Yes, a special section. The idea is that this special section will be set apart from the rest and become an instrument of the rulers. Even if its members are drawn from the ranks of the oppressed classes they are set apart from them by such things as uniforms, corporate spirit, discipline and indoctrination in the belief that it is their function to uphold 'law and order', without looking into what interests the given 'law and order' serve or how they came to be established. So long as these special armed forces remain loyal to the established state a revolution is difficult if not impossible. But as a ruling class more and more obstructs the development of the forces of production, as its rule becomes barren, discontent rises. And this discontent infects the special public force too. It becomes divided, paralyzed, or perhaps part of it goes over to the rising class. Then the state is really in danger. If the revolution is successful a new state is established.

STREETER: I can see all that and I grant that it all follows if we accept the Marxist theory of the state—that it is an instrument of the ruling class to maintain its rule. I am even prepared to grant that what you say may be true of dictatorships.

ALLEN: All states are dictatorships—dictatorships of one class over others.

STREETER: That is what you say and you may be right. I'd have to look into the question more closely to find out. But I was talking about dictatorship in our more ordinary usage of the term. According to that usage, Hitler's Germany was a dictatorship. Britain and the United States of America are not dictatorships. They are democracies.

ALLEN: Capitalist or bourgeois democracies?

STREETER: Very well, capitalist democracies if you like, but nevertheless democracies—at least in this sense: almost everyone has a vote, there is considerable freedom of discussion and organization—i.e. freedom of discussion and organization against capitalism. The government is elected by a majority of the people. You know yourself, you can vote how you please. Yet you call these capitalist states, dictatorships of the capitalist class. I don't see how you can make that out.

ALLEN: I don't want to minimize the difference between a naked dictatorship suppressing all opposition and a capitalist democracy. Nevertheless they are alike in this respect: each state is a dictatorship of capital and defends capitalist rights by force if necessary. You consider the real position in a capitalist democracy. The capitalists have the possibility of bribery direct or indirect—soft jobs for politicians who serve them and things like that. They alone have the material means to control the bulk of the mass organs of publicity, newspapers, radio, films and the like. They can finance their own organizations, pay men to see that laws are made their way and so on. With all these things in their control they can afford to allow a good deal of latitude to other people. They can do all this with perfect serenity when opposition to capitalism is not too strong. They can even afford to make concessions of some importance in themselves. But let capitalist property rights themselves be endangered by democracy and you will see that they scrap the democracy and substitute a naked dictatorship.

STREETER: Is that simply a prophecy of what will happen or can you give me some examples?

ALLEN: History has plenty of examples of this kind of

thing. If you want a recent one, consider the Hitler regime. The Weimar Republic in Germany which followed the first world war was a democracy. The inflation and then the acute depression proved that the capitalist class could no longer develop the forces of production. The discontent of the workers grew. A strong tendency to the left was discernible. With better leadership the workers' parties of Germany might have established a workers' state and expropriated the capitalists. Even as it was it was only a matter of time before that happened. The capitalists had only one course open to them—to support Hitler and his dictatorship which crushed opposition and tried to find a solution of the problem of production by foreign conquest. That is why Thyssen and Krupp and others came in behind Hitler. Of course they had to pay a heavy price but dictatorships are always costly. But it was their only path. A democracy is a better path, i.e. a cheaper one and one which is more secure and more convenient for the capitalists because it provides workable means of adjusting matters, letting off steam, rectifying minor grievances which otherwise might accumulate and so on. It is a capitalist dictatorship nevertheless.

STREETER: But look, Allen, you find that a Labour Party gets into power and it nationalizes various industries, expropriates capitalists in other words. Maybe it pays compensation but that comes to an end. If that goes far enough you'll find that your so-called capitalist state has abolished capitalism.

ALLEN: If it goes far enough but it has never gone far enough yet.

STREETER: Nevertheless the tendency is in that direction.

ALLEN: No, it isn't. You find these cases of nationalization going back a long way. Bismarck wanted to nationalize the German railways in the last century and our railways have been nationalized for years. These public utilities serve capitalists. It is better from a capitalist point of view for the costs to be spread over the whole community than for them to have to carry losses by heavy freight charges. The same sort of thing goes for the British coal mining industry. Under private ownership it was wasteful, inefficient and costly to the whole of the rest of British industry that relied upon it. No one was prepared to put up a very stiff fight about that. But let the very principle of private property in the means of production be attacked and you'll soon see a difference in the kind of resistance the ruling class puts up. There are some industries which many of the capitalists themselves would be glad to see nationalized. But that doesn't give you a workers' state. It is simply a capitalist state which itself administers some industries. And what is more, it then begins to tell the workers in those industries that they ought not to agitate for higher wages because they, the workers, now own the industries themselves. It is a gigantic swindle and as long as it will work, the capitalists don't need any naked dictatorship. They leave it to the Labour Parties to persuade the workers that they are getting somewhere, that they are on the path to the workers' state through the ballot box and the old age pension. That's the kind of thing that keeps the workers tame, keeps them from the revolutionary path, from the Marxist path of direct challenge to the Capitalist state.

CHAIRMAN: I must ask you, Allen, not to tirade.

ALLEN: I am not tirading, Mr. Chairman, I am merely explaining the Marxist position.

CHAIRMAN: Do you want any further explanation Streeter?

STREETER: Only on this point, Mr. Chairman. Do the Marxists maintain that all states are of this class character—they are simply instruments of a class?

ALLEN: No. I might answer best by a further short quotation from Engels:

. . . the modern representative state is the instrument of the exploitation of wage-labour by capital. By way of exception, however, there are periods when the warring classes so nearly attain equilibrium that the state power, ostensibly appearing as a mediator assumes for the moment a certain independence in relation to both . . .

Such a state Marxism calls a Bonapartist state after its classical representative—the regime of Napoleon Bonaparte—I mean the first Empire. Other examples would be the second Napoleonic Empire, and the Bismarck regime in Germany. A Bonapartist state can go its own way to some extent, defying the wishes of the ruling class—only so long, however, as it does not go so far as to upset the balance between the classes.

CHAIRMAN: I really must cut you short at that point Allen and ask South to speak about it.

SOUTH: Perhaps, Mr. Chairman, I would be wise to do what I have done in the past. I will tell you first of all what I agree with. Then I will take up points of disagreement. First of all I agree that what is 'order' for one social force will be 'disorder' for another. In other words we find different kinds of 'order' and the State upholds one 'order' and opposes others.

STREETER: Like capitalist 'order' against workers' 'order'.

SOUTH: That could be the kind of thing I mean. There are many others—a Roman Catholic 'order' is not the same as a Protestant 'order' or an Islamic 'order' or again a Freethinkers' 'order'; a Nazi 'order' is not the same as a democrats' 'order' and so on. You can see already that there is a difference between my view and the Marxist . . .

STREETER: You mean you don't confine yourself to classes?

SOUTH: Exactly. Nevertheless I agree there are different 'orders' in society.

STREETER: You said that was your first point of agreement. Is there any other?

SOUTH: Yes, there is. I agree as well that the state is the product of social struggles and that it is the instrument of some social forces against others.

STREETER: That is going a long way with Marxism.

SOUTH: I think it is the truth and insofar as Marxism says only so much as that, I think it is sound, but, of course, it goes further and in doing so, I think it makes serious mistakes.

STREETER: Such as?

SOUTH: Such as treating the state as an instrument of merely class domination.

STREETER: You think it is not an instrument of class domination?

SOUTH: I said it was not merely that. It is not merely that in two main ways. In the first place, there are more forces struggling in society than class forces and they can't simply be written off as reducible to class domination. You take Sabattarianism in our society. It is a strong force though it seems to be in decline now. It has been supported by the state, or rather the state has been an instrument to enforce its demands on those not giving it spontaneous adherence. Think of various laws relating to divorce, conditions of drinking alcoholic liquors, censorship on grounds of obscenity, prudery in general and so on. I don't doubt that you can show some connections between these things and economic classes but economic classes and the struggle between them don't explain them entirely. And the state is an instrument of all these things against opposing forces.

That is one way in which Marxism oversimplifies its theory of the state. And there is another way. Even if we ignore every other social force but classes it is not true to say that the state is an instrument of one class for the oppression of another. The balance between classes changes and the state expresses that balance. Even on this matter of property rights the Marxist theory of the state grossly oversimplifies.

STREETER: I think I agree with the rest of what you have said but I don't see exactly what you mean by that last point.

SOUTH: Well Allen talks as if there is some constant thing which can be called capitalist ownership of the means of production, capitalist property or something like that.

STREETER: Isn't there? It seems clear to me that there is.

SOUTH: It is clear to me that there is not. A hundred and fifty years ago we might say a capitalist owned a factory. We meant something very different from what we would mean by the same statement today. Today what safety devices he employs, the hours he works his employees, the wages he pays them, the kinds of hands he may employ for specific types of jobs, the way he markets the product and a hundred and one other things are not determined by him but by regulations or laws or rulings made by some force at least partly out of his control. There is still private property in the means of production. I am not denying that. What I am saying is that it is limited in many ways in which it was not limited 150 years ago.

STREETER: And are you saying this is good or bad?

SOUTH: I'm not dealing with the question of whether it's good or bad. That is a separate issue. The point is that it is different and this difference has been brought about partly by the fact that other forces in the state, forces apart from and often opposed to capital, have been able to use the state as their instrument to impose these limitations on private capital. That does not mean that private capital also has not used the state. It has. Both things are true. There are conflicts in society and these conflicts are expressed also in the state which is not simply the instrument of one side. It is the instrument of both sides though in different degrees at different times. And, of course, to talk about both sides is an over-simplification. There are all sorts of forces involved and these find varying degrees of expression through the state or, to put it in another way, the state is in varying degrees their instrument. Marxism gives us a neat formula but it gets its neatness at the expense of falsifying the facts.

STREETER: Would you put on one side, then, the whole Marxist theory about naked dictatorship and democracy?

SOUTH: Not the whole of it. Naked dictatorship is the product of acute social crisis, of conditions in which the hold of ruling forces is so shaky that they can't afford to risk open opposition. That much is true. It is also true that in any democracy there is a certain amount of humbug, that certain forces (and not only class forces) are in an especially favourable position to influence opinion. That certainly happens. But what I am insisting on is the plurality of kinds of forces at work, the complexity of the position. These simple formulae may be useful for getting a mass following, for bringing about certain types of political action, but they are bad political science.

STREETER: I take it then that you couldn't put your position in a neat formula.

SOUTH: Only in the most general terms. I have already given you the broad formula, 'Pluralism'. We might go further than that. If you consider an economic class like the workers—then different parts of it and different stages of it in time will be dominated by different systems of ideas. The same goes for other classes and other forces in society. So you can get a rough and ready formulation by saying that the state is the instrument of the ruling ideas in the society.

STREETER: But wouldn't you find a balance even there? I mean that you could never say that one set of ideas and one alone dominated a society. After all, you find all sorts of ideas in a given society.

SOUTH: Quite so. You get the complexity introduced by

balance and you get other complexities. You can get a state—especially a dictatorship in decline—lagging far behind the movement of ideas in the society in general. The way this all works out is very complex. That is why I say my formulation is rough and ready.

Of course you can go deeper too. You can look for the ways of life that give rise to the systems of ideas. Perhaps I could sum up my criticism of the Marxist theory of the State by saying that if you had a society without classes it would nevertheless have a state which supported some social forces against others and also expressed a balance between them. You understand that when I say a balance I don't necessarily mean an exact equilibrium. It might be very uneven.

STREETER: I understand that. But what would you say about the Marxist theory of the Bonapartist state with its degree of independence because of the equilibrium of conflicting classes?

SOUTH: I'd wipe out the confining of the conflict to the classes. Having done that I'd say that any state is to some extent Bonapartist, that is it is able to take advantage up to a point of the equilibrium between different forces to secure a certain freedom of action. The degree of this freedom of action varies of course from issue to issue. I don't think, for example, that the Australian State at the present time could abolish all censorship. The forces for censorship are too strong for that. On the other hand I don't think it could ban all except Government publications. The forces against that would be too strong. And we have to take into account not merely forces for or against censorship but also forces wishing to express a particular point of view though quite willing to be censorious otherwise, commercial interests and a host of others. Even so within limits there is some elbow room for the state in Australia in this matter of censorship. It is mainly an instrument of a certain complicated balance. Nevertheless it can manoeuvre a little.

STREETER: I see. I think your views of the State are sounder than the Marxist ones.

ALLEN: That is because you have been exposed to so much capitalist propaganda.

CHAIRMAN: Well, we'd better end there.

V

Ideology

CHAIRMAN: Well, gentlemen, we have discussed Marxist philosophy, the Marxist theory of history, the theory of class struggle, and the theory of the state. When we were discussing the theory of history, you were repeatedly breaking away to discuss ideology. Tonight I am going to invite you to concentrate on that subject of ideology . . .

STREETER: On the Marxist theory of ideology?

CHAIRMAN: On the Marxist theory of ideology. I shall as usual ask Allen to expound the Marxist view. South may later make any criticisms he wishes to make. And you Streeter, of course, may intervene at any point.

STREETER: Haven't we already had something on this subject? I don't mean what we said ourselves. Didn't we have a quotation from Marx about it?

ALLEN: Yes, we did. What you are thinking about is the quotation from Marx's Introduction to his *Critique of Political-Economy*. That quotation sums up his theory of history and part of this theory concerns ideology.

STREETER: That's right, but I forget what he had to say about it. I remember he said that there was an economic foundation and that determines the superstructure of society which includes ideology. But that doesn't tell us what ideology is. What is it?

ALLEN: That is not easy to answer. Perhaps the best approach to it, is to recall exactly what Marx said in that passage. You are quite right in what you remember about the economic foundation and the superstructure which includes ideology. You may remember that he said that 'it is not the consciousness of men which determines their existence, but on the contrary it is their social existence which determines their consciousness.' He goes on to describe how a social revolution takes place. The economic foundation changes:

With the change in the economic foundation the whole immense superstructure is slowly or rapidly transformed. In studying such a transformation one must always distinguish between the material transformation in the economic conditions essential to production—which can be established with the exactitude of natural science—and the juridical, political, religious, artistic, or philosophic, in short ideological forms, in which men become conscious of this conflict and fight it out. As little as one judges what an individual is by what he thinks of himself, so little can one judge such an epoch of transformation by its consciousness; one must rather explain this consciousness by the contradictions in the material life, the conflict at hand between the social forces of production and the relations in which production is carried on.

STREETER: That certainly is difficult. It seems to me that Marx is saying that men think they are fighting about one thing when in fact they are fighting about something else. Is that correct? Then what they think would be their ideology wouldn't it?

ALLEN: That is correct.

STREETER: Does Marx give any examples?

ALLEN: Yes, he does. I will give you one of them. In his book, *The Eighteenth Brumaire of Louis Bonaparte*, he writes:

As in private life we distinguish between what a man thinks and says about himself, and what he really is and does, still more in historical struggles we must distinguish the phrases and imaginations of parties from their real organism and their real interests . . . Thus the Tories in England long imagined that they were raving about the Kingdom, the Church, and the Beauty of the Old-English dispensation, until the day of danger snatched from them the confession that they were only raving about the Ground Rent.

STREETER: That means that all their talk about the Kingdom, the Church and the Beauty of the Old-English dispensation—all that was ideology?

ALLEN: Exactly, but don't think that it is merely a matter of talk. Marx does not mean that they were deliberately telling lies. Marx means that they really believed these things. They really believed they were defending the King and the Church and the Old-English Dispensation.

STREETER: How do you know that Marx meant that?

ALLEN: There is plenty of evidence I might quote. There is even sufficient in the quotations I have given you. Marx says it is men's 'social existence which determines their consciousness.' And again he speaks of 'the ideological forms in which men become conscious of this conflict and fight it out.' I think it is clear enough that he is thinking about what men *believe* and not only about what they *say*. You'll notice he has the same line of thought in the second passage. He talks about 'what a man thinks and says' not only about what a man says, and he also talks about 'the phrases and imaginations of parties' not only about their phrases. I can't see much room for doubt as to his meaning. An ideology is not a set of lies which men deliberately make up. It is a set of beliefs which they come to hold quite sincerely.

STREETER: I concede you the point. It does seem clear that that is what Marx meant.

ALLEN: There is no doubt about it. Engels is even more explicit. In his *letter to Conrad Schmidt* of October 27th, 1890, Engels wrote that

The reflection of economic relations in the form of legal principles is accomplished in such a way that this process does not reach the consciousness of the agent. The law maker imagines that he is acting from a priori principles, when in reality it is all a matter of economic reflection . . . and that distortion, when it is not conscious, we call the ideological outlook.

And again in his book on *Feuerbach* he writes: 'That the material conditions of life of the men in whose heads this thinking process takes place, ultimately determines the course of the process, necessarily remains unknown to these men, otherwise there would be an end of the whole ideology.'

STREETER: Don't bother to argue that point any more. I'm completely satisfied about what they meant—at least as far as beliefs and mere statements are concerned. I can see that men believe their ideologies. But does this mean that everything we believe is ideology or is an ideology one kind of thinking only? I mean is there any other kind of thinking, is there some thinking which is not ideological?

ALLEN: That is a difficult question.

STREETER: Is it really so difficult? I have been thinking

about the quotations you have given us and I think they give us the answer.

CHAIRMAN: Go ahead, Streeter. Give us the answer if you think it is there.

STREETER: Of course it is there. It is becoming quite obvious the more I think about it. You remember the first quotation from Marx that Allen gave us. In that Marx made a distinction. He said that 'one must always distinguish between the material transformation in the economic conditions . . . which can be established with the exactitude of natural science . . .'—notice that—'which can be established with the exactitude of natural science'. One must always distinguish, Marx says, between that on the one hand and, on the other hand the 'ideological forms in which men become conscious of this conflict and fight it out.'

Surely he is making a clear distinction between natural science on the one hand and ideology on the other. What men think they are fighting about—that is ideology. But the real changes can be found out—and that is science. After all Marx himself claims to be telling us what is true. He claims that his account of society is scientific. If it isn't, if it is ideology, the same as all other accounts, then why should we bother with it?

SOUTH: Good for you, Streeter. I think you've hit the bull's eye.

CHAIRMAN: Please hold your comments, South, until later. Do you think you can support your theory Streeter from the other quotations?

STREETER: Of course I can. In the second quotation Marx says that 'we distinguish what a man thinks and says about himself, and what he really is and does.' So apparently we can know what he really is and does. That is science. What he thinks about himself is ideology. Similarly Marx assumes that we can know the real organisms and the real interests of parties. That is science. But their phrases and imaginations are ideology. It is in his example too. The Tories thought they were raving about Kingdom, Church and so on. That was their ideology. But really they were raving about ground rent. Marx knows that and it is science.

CHAIRMAN: So you are saying that Marxism makes a distinction between ideology and science?

STREETER: Exactly. I think there is no doubt about it and what is more I agree with the distinction.

CHAIRMAN: Well Allen, what have you to say about that?

ALLEN: The matter is not as simple as Streeter thinks. He is forgetting important aspects of Marxism when he attributes his interpretation to Marx. He is even forgetting part of the quotation from Marx which I gave him. Marx said that it is men's 'social existence which determines their consciousness.' What men think is determined by their social existence. If that is true it does away with the distinction that Streeter thinks he sees between science and ideology.

STREETER: That can't possibly be right. Marxism itself is supposed to be scientific. If it is, as you say, simply an ideology like other ideologies, why should we bother with it?

ALLEN: Marxists are not in the least upset by the assertion that Marxism is an ideology. I can illustrate that point by quotations from many leading Marxists. Rosa Luxemburg, for example, wrote in an article on the twentieth anniversary of the death of Marx:

'Marxism pretends only to temporary truth; dialectic through and through, it contains within itself the seeds of its own destruction.'

Lenin in *One Step Forward, Two Steps Back* speaks of Marxism as 'the ideology of the proletariat instructed by capitalism.' Trotsky in *Terrorism and Communism* writes that 'in the socialist movement ideology plays its essential and enormous role.'

I could go on multiplying quotations like these. Those people were Marxists. It did not daunt them in the least to recognize Marxism as an ideology.

STREETER: But surely it must. They are claiming that Marxism is scientific.

ALLEN: You are talking as if science itself was something immutable and eternal. Plekhanov has dealt with this very point. In his Preface to the Russian translation of Engels' *Socialism Utopian and Scientific*, he writes:

Human society in its development passes through certain phases to which correspond certain phases of development of social science. That which we call, for example, bourgeois economics is one phase of development of economic science. That which we call socialist economics is another phase of its development immediately following . . .

The bourgeois economics, in so far as it corresponds to a definite phase of social evolution, possesses scientific truth. But that truth is relative, exactly because it corresponds only to a certain phase of social development. The bourgeois theoreticians, imagining that society must always remain in its bourgeois phase, attribute absolute significance to that relative truth. In that consists their fundamental mistake, corrected by scientific socialism, the appearance of which testifies that the bourgeois epoch of social development is nearing its end.

STREETER: And you are saying that scientific socialism itself possesses only relative truth, that at a certain phase of history it too will need to be corrected.

ALLEN: Exactly. Scientific socialism reflects only the period of the class struggle, the final period of the class struggle, the struggle between capital and labour. It is true for that period. When that period is over and the classless society comes into being then it will be superseded. A new phase of social science will come into being, not a class science, this time but a truly human science.

STREETER: So you think that when Marx talks about establishing something with the exactitude of natural science he is using science in that sense, in a relative sense?

ALLEN: Of course. How else could he use it? If he meant that it could be established absolutely and eternally he wouldn't be a Marxist, he'd be adopting a bourgeois standpoint. He'd be making the same mistake that Plekhanov points out in the case of the bourgeois scientists.

STREETER: So you're saying that all science is ideology.

ALLEN: That is so.

STREETER: Then what distinction does Marx think he is making? After all he does say 'one must always distinguish'. Distinguish what? One ideology from another? If so why doesn't he say that? Instead he says 'science' on the one hand, 'ideology' on the other hand.

ALLEN: He could say 'one ideology from another'. But don't forget that the ideology which he expresses is the proletarian ideology, the ideology of scientific socialism, the one which possesses validity in our day, in the period of the struggle between capital and labour. So in our period this is science, this is objective truth in the sense of the nearest approach to ultimate truth that has yet been made.

STREETER: Who says so? These ideologists themselves? If so what guarantee have we that their ideology is nearer the mark than any other?

ALLEN: In practice man proves the truth of his theory.

STREETER: Well we can't wait now for practice to settle that issue, but I'd like to raise another issue. You spoke a moment ago as if ideologies always belonged to classes.

ALLEN: That is so. Speaking in broad terms there is a feudal ideology i.e. the ideology which is a reflection of the nature and social position of the rulers of feudal society; there is a capitalist or bourgeois ideology; there is a proletarian ideology and so on.

STREETER: That seems over simple to me. After all, we do find differences in ideas in one social class.

ALLEN: Of course we do. A class is a very complex thing. Different sections of the capitalist class, for example, have different ways of working according to the peculiarities of their function in production—and different interests up to a point. I might mention, in a broad way, industrial capital and finance capital. That will mean differences in ideology, shadings we might call them. Nevertheless, just as the bourgeoisie of whatever type has certain interests in common, namely property interests, so their ideology has certain features in common in virtue of which we should call it all bourgeois ideology.

STREETER: That would need to be checked in detail.

ALLEN: I realize that, but it is impossible to say everything now. I will mention one other point. We do find members of one class adopting the ideology of another.

STREETER: I was just thinking that. Engels was a capitalist and yet he claimed to believe proletarian ideology. How do you account for that?

ALLEN: It is not only phenomena like that which we need to explain. It is also that many workers adopt a bourgeois ideology.

STREETER: Yes, of course that is true. Well, how do you explain it?

ALLEN: While the bourgeoisie, the capitalists, are the ruling class, while they are firmly seated in the saddle, they are developing the productive forces of society, they are capable of playing a progressive role. They are also still struggling against and eliminating remnants of former ruling systems. In so far as they are doing these things they have a certain common interest with the proletariat which is also a progressive class and which is therefore receptive at that stage, to bourgeois ideas. Besides, the bourgeoisie as the ruling class has command of propaganda instruments on a colossal scale. This too helps to get its ideas accepted by the proletariat or some members of the proletariat. Besides when a class is the ruling class and is flourishing this means that all the institutions of society are shaped and run in the way it wants them and in accordance with its ideas. Within these institutions the ruled have to live. So they imbibe the ideas. Besides there is a certain inertia about changes in the superstructure. Ideas linger on for a time. They don't change in a flash with changes in the economic foundation but only gradually. It is true that the seeds of conflict between bourgeoisie and proletariat are there from the beginning and, in the proletariat, the germs of its own ideology are present. But they take time to develop. And they don't flourish until the proletariat has developed its own institutions, until the new society has grown to a considerable extent within the old.

STREETER: I see that. What about the other way round—a capitalist like Engels with proletarian ideology, even a pioneer of it?

ALLEN: In such cases the individual's understanding of the whole historic process, of the transience of the rule of his own class and of the inevitability of the triumph of the oppressed class, leads him to identify himself with them, with the oppressed, and to adopt their ideology, even to become conscious of it before they do themselves.

CHAIRMAN: I must stop you there, Allen. I know there is much more you can say on the subject. There always is for all of us, but we must give South his chance to criticize.

SOUTH: Thank you, Mr. Chairman. I think I'll begin with Streeter's points. I agree with them entirely. When Marx says that the Tories were interested in ground rent he means that in fact they were interested in ground rent. If he was right on that point, if those Tories about whom he was writing, really were interested in ground rent then that never will be superseded. It is a fact. It is science. And it always will be true that the Tories of 18th and 19th century England were interested in ground rent. And if Marx was wrong, if they weren't interested in ground rent, then it certainly is not true relative to his period or class or any other period or class. It might be said that it would help the proletariat if it believed that it was true. If that is a fact then it simply means that belief in a falsehood helps the proletariat. It does not mean that the statement is true for the proletariat or possesses a relative truth. That would certainly lead us straight to the subjectivism about which Lenin was so scornful.

STREETER: I thought it was clear that Marx meant that. Do you agree with me then that Marx does distinguish science and ideology?

SOUTH: I certainly do. When Marx says that you can establish 'the material transformation in the economic conditions . . . with the exactitude of natural science' he means exactly what he says. He means that certain transformations occur and that we can know what they are. This is science. There is nothing relative about it. We are either right or wrong. And if we are right, it is meaningless to talk about our view being superseded. If we are wrong, we are just plain wrong and not right for our own class or something like that. Ideology on the other hand is wrong. It is, as Engels says, a 'distortion'.

STREETER: What is ideology then?

SOUTH: You'll remember that you asked Allen that question. He did not answer it. He could not answer it except by saying that it is all thinking. That is what follows from the Marxist position.

STREETER: But you just said that Marx did not say that, that Marx distinguishes science from ideology. Then you were agreeing with me against Allen. Now you are agreeing with Allen against me.

SOUTH: Both things are true—I mean that Marx adopts both positions although they are inconsistent with each other. The position that you recognized in Marx is the one, I think, which is valuable for social and political science. Men adopt beliefs which suit the interests of the social forces to which they belong. They adopt these beliefs, not because that is how the facts really are, but because it suits those interests to believe that that is how the facts really are. We are all familiar with wishful thinking in individual cases. Marx has stressed the existence of wishful thinking on a social scale. In doing this he has rendered a great service to social and political science. Ideologies are an important part of history and much about them that we could not otherwise understand we can explain by approaching them in a Marxist way and seeing them as believed because they serve certain interests.

STREETER: But there is still science?

SOUTH: Yes, there is still science. There is wishful thinking or ideological thinking but there is not only this kind of thinking. There is also recognition of facts or scientific thinking. It is this which enables us to give an account of ideology itself.

STREETER: What do you say then about Marx's assertion that social existence determines consciousness.

SOUTH: Where you have ideological thinking then what Marx says is true. It is also true that only people of a certain kind are able to recognize what certain facts really are. In that sense what Marx says is true even of scientific thinking. But granted the receptivity then consciousness is determined by the facts. If you put a piece of green paper in front of me, tell me it is either blue or green and ask me what colour it is, then if I desperately want it to be blue I may say and believe 'Blue'. Here my existence has determined my consciousness. But if I have no such obstruction to my perception then my consciousness will be determined by the actual colour of the paper. I will say and believe 'Green'. If you change it to blue I will perceive the change.

STREETER: That seems reasonable to me although your example is a crude one.

SOUTH: Not crude, merely familiar and easy to grasp. The same principle applies in the case of complex bodies of doctrine. The ideologies for which men believe they fight work on the same sort of principle. It suits certain interests to believe these doctrines. Hence they are believed though the real facts are quite otherwise.

STREETER: You agree with Allen then that men believe their ideologies.

SOUTH: Oh yes. I do agree with him that Marx thought that and I further agree that it is so. Mind you there are men who make use of an ideology. They don't believe it themselves but they profess to do so in order to gain their own ends. But this is possible only because there are people who do believe it.

STREETER: And do you think that Marxism itself is an ideology or is it science?

SOUTH: Parts of Marxist doctrine are science, parts are ideology. For example when Marx asserts that there are ideologies then that is scientific. He is observing the facts that are there. But in other parts of his doctrine which I have criticized he is being ideological. He is putting forward beliefs which he holds because they serve certain interests with which he has identified himself. For example the dialectic I think is definitely ideological. It is nonsensical in itself but was kept by Marx partly to support his theory of class struggle, partly to help him over other difficulties. Even mixed in with that, of course, there is some truth e.g. that things are in flux, that there are conflicts, that what comes into being also passes away and so on. My view is that in studying Marxism from a scientific point of view we have to separate out the truth that is in it, amend Marxist assertions that get near the truth or hint at the truth and discard the mistakes, the ideological elements.

STREETER: And do you agree that ideologies are class ideologies?

SOUTH: No, I don't. This really goes back to my criticism of the class struggle theory. If you want to get the full force of my argument you'll have to go back to that script. You may remember that I denied that classes were the only historical forces. It is not simply a matter of complexity within classes as Allen says although that occurs too. It is also a matter of different ways of life that we find in society. These different ways of life have their interests and consequently ideologies can grow up attached to those interests, supported by those interests, i.e. believed because they serve those interests. If you could get a classless society I think you'd still get a clash of ideologies. I'm saying then that ideologies are attached to various ways of life and not simply to classes.

STREETER: That means you'd give a different explanation

from Allen for the fact that a capitalist like Engels could adopt a proletarian ideology.

SOUTH: You're right there. But I would not accept the description of Marxism as a proletarian ideology. It did not arise from the workers. Indeed Lenin says that the workers are incapable of developing it, that it has to be brought to them from the outside by bourgeois intellectuals. His reason for calling it a proletarian ideology is that he believes it is in the interest of the workers. The fact that they did not develop it themselves should have made him suspect that fact. My view is that it takes in many workers because it flatters them as the class with the great historic mission, because it paints a rosy future for them, and because it sides with them in opposition to the capitalist boss. Actually it is an ideology which serves the interests of those who want to see society run in a certain direction by people like themselves—planners of society if you like to call them that—in any case intellectuals discontented with existing society. Engels accepted it and developed it because he was that kind of man. So did Marx or Lenin or Trotsky or any of the great Marxists. They were not workers nor was their ideology a workers' ideology. They were against capitalism and they saw the workers as a force that could overthrow capitalism. I don't mean that Engels did not sincerely believe that the revolution would be in the workers' interests. He did believe this. So did the others. But as he himself points out, holders of ideologies are taken in by their ideologies, are not conscious of the real forces at work. You might say that Marxism is an ideology for bureaucrats and all the great Marxists are the product of bureaucratic societies.

STREETER: You say that this explanation is sound and Allen's wrong. You may be right but you have only given us an alternative. You haven't shown that Allen's explanation is false.

SOUTH: Allen's explanation breaks down of itself. What a man thinks is determined by what he is. That is what Allen says. Yet here is Engels who is a capitalist and son of a capitalist who thinks in an allegedly proletarian manner. It won't stand up. Allen's explanation is that this was because Engels understood the historical process as a whole. But how could he if his social existence determined his consciousness? He could come to such understanding only if that process itself could impinge upon his consciousness and determine what he thought in spite of his social existence which for Marxism means his class position. Actually, though a capitalist and son of a capitalist, he was able to think in an anti-capitalist manner because history is more complex than a struggle between classes. It is for example also a struggle between philosophical schools. And Engels happened to fall in with the Hegelian philosophical school, in particular with the young Hegelians who were being critical in the sphere of religion, politics and in many other respects. In other words ideologies themselves caught young Engels and carried him along. And the same applies to Marx. It is interesting to notice that the workers and socialism don't come into Marx's oppositional activities until he has already made his mark as an oppositional figure. But my main point is that if you consider Engels purely from a class point of view you can never explain how he got to understand anything but a capitalist ideology.

CHAIRMAN: I really must stop you there South and also the discussion.

VI

Religion

CHAIRMAN: Gentlemen, last time we discussed the Marxist theory of ideology. I thought that we might follow up that discussion by talking about Religion. We have referred to it from time to time in our other discussions. I would be right, wouldn't I, Allen, in saying that for Marxism it is a particular branch of ideology and is determined by the economic basis of society?

ALLEN: Yes, Mr. Chairman, that is correct. In *The German Ideology*, Marx and Engels write that

Morality, religion, metaphysics, and ideology in general, with their appropriate forms of consciousness, thus forfeit the semblance of independence. They have no history, no evolution, of their own. Human beings, developing material production and material intercourse, and thus altering the real world that environs them, alter therewith their own thought and the products of their thought. Consciousness does not determine life, but life determines consciousness.

We may add that quotation to the others I have given before to remove any doubts about the way in which Marxism regards ideology in general and religion in particular.

STREETER: That is all very well, Allen, but it does not get us any further forward. Have Marx and Engels nothing to say specifically about religion?

ALLEN: Yes, they have. I think Marx's attitude is well summed up in his *Theses on Feuerbach* and also in certain passages in his *Introduction to a Critique of the Hegelian Philosophy of Right*. I think it might be more easily understood if I quoted from the latter. I might add a short passage or two from the *Theses on Feuerbach* to round out the picture.

CHAIRMAN: Very well, let us have the passages from the *Introduction to a Critique of the Hegelian Philosophy of Right*.
ALLEN: Marx wrote:

Man makes religion; religion does not make man. Religion, indeed, is the self-consciousness and the self-feeling of the man who either has not yet found himself, or else (having found himself) has lost himself once more. But man is not an abstract being, squatting down somewhere outside the world. Man is the world of men, the State, society. This State, this society, produce religion, produce a perverted world consciousness, because they are a perverted world. Religion is the generalised theory of this world, its encyclopaedic compend, its logic in a popular form . . . The fight against religion is, therefore, a direct campaign against the world whose spiritual aroma is religion.

Religion is the sigh of the oppressed creature, the feelings of a heartless world, just as it is the spirit of unspiritual conditions. It is the opium of the people.

The people cannot be really happy until it has been deprived of illusory happiness by the abolition of religion. The demand that the people should shake itself free of illusion as to its own condition is the demand that it should abandon a condition which needs illusion.

Thus, it is the mission of history, after the other-worldly truth has disappeared, to establish the truth of this world. In the next place, it is the mission of philosophy, having entered into the service of history after the true nature of the reputed sainthood of human self-estrangement has been disclosed, to disclose all the unsaintliness of this self-estrangement. Thus the criticism of heaven is transformed into a criticism of earth, the criticism of religion into a criticism of law, the criticism of theology into a criticism of politics.

And in the same work he says that

The criticism of religion ends with the doctrine that man is the highest being for man; it ends, that is to say, with the categorical imperative that all conditions must be revolutionised in which man is a debased, an enslaved, an abandoned, a contemptible being.

CHAIRMAN: And what about the *Theses on Feuerbach*? Do you want to add anything from those?
ALLEN: I don't know that it is necessary. In the theses Marx

is insisting on the same points. He regards Feuerbach as not having pressed his criticism of religion far enough. He says in thesis 6: 'Feuerbach resolves the essence of religion into the human essence. But the human essence is not an abstraction inherent in the isolated individual. In its reality, it is the totality of social relations. . . .' And again in thesis 7 he says: 'Feuerbach, therefore, does not see that the "religious sentiment" is itself a social product, and the abstract individual he analyses belongs to a determinate social form.'

STREETER: To what part of Marx's life do these statements belong?

ALLEN: They are in early works—1844 and 1845.

STREETER: Did he change his opinion about them?

ALLEN: No. I know of no evidence that he did. He may have put some of his phrases differently had he written them at a later date, but the main outlines certainly belong to the permanent Marxist system. These passages are certainly in harmony with his mature work. In one place he later went deeper.

STREETER: Which place is that?

ALLEN: Well, he would always have maintained that 'the criticism of heaven is transformed into a criticism of earth', but later he would have insisted that the 'criticism of earth' meant basically not the criticism of law and politics but, in the last instance, the criticism of economic structure.

STREETER: Yes, I see that would be so. Could I have a look at those quotations? There were some points I did not grasp.

ALLEN: Certainly.

STREETER: I did not understand this point about 'the man who has not yet found himself' or who 'has lost himself'.

ALLEN: Marx is referring to the man who is not truly human, the man who has been dehumanized by his social conditions. In a class society we have not truly human individuals. Neither oppressors nor oppressed are truly human. The world is, as Marx says, 'heartless'. So it finds its 'heart', its 'feelings' in another world, a world of illusion. The 'truly human man' doesn't need opium or the consolations of illusions. He can live in reality because reality is acceptable. But that can happen only where reality is acceptable, where it does not need illusions to make it bearable.

STREETER: I think I see his meaning. He means that if we can revolutionize conditions in which 'man is a debased, an enslaved, an abandoned, a contemptible being', if we can do that then that will be the end of religion.

ALLEN: Exactly.

STREETER: But suppose we can't revolutionize conditions, then does that not mean that mere criticism of religion won't succeed in abolishing it? If the revolution does not happen then religion will go on.

ALLEN: That is so. Marx says in his eleventh thesis on Feuerbach—'Philosophers have done nothing more than interpret the world in various ways; our business is to change it.' Changing the world is the philosopher's proper business. It is a radical form of criticism. This is the only way in which religious illusions can be wiped out. However, don't forget that elsewhere Marx proved that the revolution was inevitable.

STREETER: Isn't Marx making an assumption in all this talk about religion?

ALLEN: No doubt he is making several assumptions, but what specific assumption have you in mind?

STREETER: That religious beliefs are false.

ALLEN: That is certainly so. They are illusions.

STREETER: Surely he needs to demonstrate that.

ALLEN: Not necessarily. Marx is not writing in isolation. He is basing his work on thinking that has been done by other men—in particular, Feuerbach. Accepting Feuerbach's thesis that religion is man-made, he is surely entitled to go on from there and point out that 'man' has to be understood in a social, not a purely individual sense. Moreover, don't forget the relativity of truth to social conditions.

CHAIRMAN: Do you want to ask any questions, South?

SOUTH: No, Mr. Chairman, I think I understand the Marxist position on religion. But I think it is a pity that Allen did not give us Marx's fourth thesis on Feuerbach. I think that gives us additional information on Marx's theory.

ALLEN: Yes, I think it would fill out the picture. I did not want to go on for too long with quotations that merely repeat points, but perhaps the fourth thesis would fill in detail. Anyway, here it is:

Feuerbach sets out from the fact of religious self-alienation, and the duplication of the world into a religious world and a mundane one. His work consists in reducing the religious world to its mundane foundation. If the mundane foundation lifts itself above itself and establishes itself in an independent realm in the clouds, that is only to be explained as an outcome of the dismemberment and self-contradictoriness of this mundane foundation. The mundane foundation must, therefore, be understood as practically revolutionised both in itself and in its contradictions. Thus as soon as the earthly family has been revealed as the mystery of the holy family, the former must itself be annihilated both theoretically and practically.

STREETER: What on earth does that mean?

ALLEN: Well, firstly the real world, this world, is deeply divided—dismembered, self-contradictory.

STREETER: Yes, I see that.

ALLEN: Secondly, it projects a picture of itself 'into the clouds'. The content of religious beliefs is given by social conditions. A feudal society with its hierarchy will result in a hierarchical order in heaven.

STREETER: But if men are dissatisfied with the real world, why repeat it in heaven?

SOUTH: But they don't repeat it exactly. Their religious beliefs reproduce its main features only, with the strife and the unsatisfactory side wiped out. Heaven compensates for the deficiencies of the real world by adding to all the divisions of the real world a spurious unity, a reconciliation. That is how I understand the Marxist theory of religion. Religious beliefs contain the real world, but expressed in a mythological way, and also with the unsatisfactory features made satisfactory, justified.

ALLEN: I agree with that. I think it is what Marx means when he talks on the one hand of religion being 'the generalised theory of this world' and on the other hand, of religion being 'the feelings of a heartless world', 'the spirit of unspiritual conditions', 'the opium of the people.' It is not merely something that takes people's mind off the world as it is. It justifies the world as it is.

CHAIRMAN: I think it is time we considered some criticisms of this Marxist theory. Do you have any to offer, South?

SOUTH: I don't know that I am going to put up much in opposition to Marx on this subject, Mr. Chairman. I agree with him that religious beliefs are false, I agree that they arise out of social conflict, I agree that they seek to make a situation of conflict tolerable by giving it a spurious unity, I agree that changed social conditions produce changed religious beliefs.

STREETER: Don't you disagree with Marx at any point?

SOUTH: Yes, I do. I don't agree that it is class division which is fundamental to the existence of religious belief. That is one division which may be involved but it is not the only one. However, I have argued that point before, when we were talking about the class struggle, and I won't repeat my points now.

STREETER: You mean that if we accept your criticism of the Marxist theory of class struggle, we will say that religion arises out of social conflicts of various kinds and not merely out of class conflicts?

SOUTH: That is correct. And I don't agree either that religion is going to come to an end. It will always be a feature of human society. But that is because I don't believe that deep social conflicts come to an end. I think we might more appropriately discuss that point when we come to consider Marx's notion of the inevitability of the classless society. I have already said something about it when we were discussing the alleged upward path of history.

STREETER: You mean that if history does not follow an upward path there is no reason for thinking religion must come to an end?

SOUTH: Quite so. I might mention another point, but this is not so much a matter of disagreement with Marx. It is merely a matter of supplementing him. I think we can raise the question of a psychological explanation of religion. Freud has attempted something of the kind in suggesting, very broadly speaking, that God is an infantile image of the father. I think it is not difficult to use this theory or something like it, and the social explanation as complementary explanations. I don't think I had better expand that.

CHAIRMAN: No, I'm afraid it would lead us off the track.

SOUTH: I'll say only this, to indicate the kind of thing I mean. If the adult emotional relations to God are akin to the infantile relations to the father, and if the infantile image of the father does supply us with some of the attributes of

God—omnipotence, love, awefulness and so on—nevertheless, there remains the question of God's moral commands and these arise I suggest out of the demands of social forces. Similarly the theories of the nature of the heavenly order in general have a social origin, as Marx says.

CHAIRMAN: Is there any other point you want to make?

SOUTH: Yes, Mr. Chairman—just this one. It is very difficult but I think it ought to be made. There is a sense in which I disagree with Marx when he says religion has no history of its own. If we accept his view that religion is a disguised kind of social theory—with distortions as he says—then it follows that it is possible to get a certain continuity. If theologians, without knowing what they are doing, are really theorizing about society in a mythological way (or even about psychology), then we can have continuity—the testing and rejecting of earlier theories while retaining certain aspects of them, the dealing with the same problems because they are real problems and making use of the work that has been done before. Theories about 'grace' strike me as of that kind. 'Grace' is treated as a theological matter, whereas it is actually a social phenomenon. We can find a history of theory of such things then, even though it is expressed in theological terms.

STREETER: Mr. Chairman, I want to protest about all this. I was led to believe that South was an opponent of Marxism. On other issues he has opposed it. As far as I'm concerned, I don't care a fig how important the economic structure is, or whether there is a class struggle or other struggles besides class struggles, or whether various kinds of thinking are ideology or science and all those things that South has been making such a fuss about. I don't say that they are not important enough in their place, but they are trivial compared with the issue that is before us tonight. To me the important thing, the most important thing, the 'basis' if you like, is God, and here is South who is supposed to disagree with Marx and on this point you can hardly tell the difference between him and Marx. 'A psychological explanation as well as a social explanation', 'religion has a history because it is really social theory', 'the conflicts leading to religious beliefs are not only class conflicts' and all the rest of it. All that is to Marxism as Tweedledum to Tweedledee.

CHAIRMAN: I must remind you, Streeter, that South is quite entitled to express his own views. He is in general opposition to some of the main Marxist theories. It does not follow that he must oppose Marx on every point. But if you feel there is some important issue that is not being treated, you are quite at liberty to bring it out.

STREETER: I certainly do feel that there is an important issue that is not being treated. Moreover, I maintain that most of the Marxist discussion of religion (and South's too) is completely beside the point. Here they are straining theories to find out why men believe in God whereas the answer is perfectly plain. Men believe in God because God exists. Once you accept the existence of God then all this other talk is beside the point.

ALLEN: No doubt it would be if God existed, but his existence would need to be demonstrated and that is beyond anybody. Besides, the ideological nature of theories of God are clearly demonstrable by the way in which they change with changing social conditions.

STREETER: Even if we grant changing conceptions of God, there is nothing in that to show he doesn't exist. Man once believed the earth was a disc, then a cylinder, then a sphere, then a cylinder again and later a sphere again. I've forgotten all the variations and the right order, but you know the kind of thing I mean. There have been all sorts of theories about the earth. Are you going to say that that shows the ideological nature of theories of the earth? It shows that at least some of the theories (perhaps all of them) have ideological elements in them, but nevertheless the earth is there. Men have been thinking about something real, even if they've made mistakes.

SOUTH: Yes, but the earth is observable. God is not.

STREETER: I don't agree. I don't agree with either of your assertions. We may be able to observe bits of the earth; we can't observe its shape. We can only deduce its shape from what we can observe. In the same sense in which we can observe the earth, we can observe God. We may not see him or feel him but we can experience him. I have experienced God myself. And we can observe his workings in the lives of men and in nature. We can observe the strength that comes from prayer, from communion with God, and we can observe the design in nature and from that deduce a designer, namely God.

CHAIRMAN: Assuming this to be so, will you relate it to Marxist theory, Streeter?

STREETER: Yes, certainly I will. Since God exists and men can know that he exists, and since he has his commands for men, certain things follow.

First, you don't have to explain by reference to infantile images or social conflicts why men believe in God. They believe because they perceive the truth—just as in the case of South's 'green' paper or 'blue' paper or whatever it was in our earlier discussion. He believed it was green because that was its real colour and he perceived it.

Second, since God exists, religion (in the sense of religious theory) can have its own history just as much as can social theory. We can find men's knowledge of God developing. And what they know influences their conduct and so the kind of society they live in and the kind of men they are. Religion makes man.

Of course I know man makes religion too, but that is false religion. You can use all your psychological and sociological factors to explain that. I am not denying that wishful thinking and ideology play their part in thinking about religion. They do, I know they do. Men do conceive God in their own image or in the image of their social idols. I know they do. But you show me a branch of science in which that does not happen and then, but only then, I'll admit that that is a good and sufficient reason for giving up belief in God. Whatever mistakes men make about God, it doesn't alter the fact that He is.

Third, man's practice flows from God's existence and His moral commands insofar as men have perceived them. No doubt the world has its influence too—the world or, as South and Allen would no doubt say, 'Society'. That has its influence and leads men away from God. But we can't simply ignore God and treat Him as if He were not a force in history.

Fourth, the more truly human a man is the less he is 'debased', 'enslaved', 'abandoned', or 'contemptible', the more clearly he will perceive God, the stronger will religion be in him.

Fifth, it is a consequence of this fourth point that if you could have a revolution which made men more truly human, it would strengthen religion, not weaken it.

Sixth, I think it is pure ideology on Allen's part to imagine you are going to get this society which is not divided by serious conflict. If he or his master, Marx, had listened more to the teachings of religion, he would have learned that evil is part of the nature of man and that it is this evil in the heart that makes the cleavages among men. It can be overcome only to the degree to which the individual puts himself into the hands of God. And we know from history that men won't do that on the grand scale. The world occasionally gets a little better and sometimes worse. There are ups and downs. And because men in the mass won't turn to God, won't do the one thing that can make them truly human, the world is unsatisfactory for them and so they develop superstitions about the one thing needful to make a perfect world—they need only abolish the aristocracy, or they need only abolish capitalism, or they need only set up a republic, or wipe out slavery, or establish the classless society or do some other such thing and there men will be truly human. It is all superstition. They wade through rivers of blood and carry loads of misery, and hatred, and desperate striving and where are they when they've finished? Disillusioned, disappointed, still with their cleavages but still ready to swallow the next superstition that comes along. The worst superstitions are the apparently secular superstitions that pride themselves on being very scientific. And it is inevitable that it should be so because those who hold them have turned furthest away from reliance on God. The Marxists talk about belief in God arising from unsatisfactory relations among men and they call that ideological. Let me tell you that you get really ideological beliefs like this one about the classless society—it's a dream, pure wishful thinking—you get that sort of ideology arising from unsatisfactory relations among men which, in their turn, are due to unsatisfactory relations with God.

SOUTH: That is turning the tables on us, Allen, with a vengeance.

STREETER: It is not turning the tables at all, South. This is no mere retort. Religious men have been hammering at this point ever since there was human society. But the children of this world are wiser in their own generation than the children of light. They think they know better. They have a remedy—a secular remedy—for the ills of the world and away they go and try it. They all prove what fools their predecessors were and how they are superior. It is left to their successors to wonder how they could be so foolish. I have been very patient through all these discussions. I don't pretend to have made a careful study of Marxism. I have been content to try to help your discussions by asking a layman's questions but I refuse to sit here silent when I hear you discuss religion on the tacit assumption that it is false, and when I hear you say that Marx believed that all preceding revolutionaries did *not* know what they were doing whereas the Marxists *did* know what *they* were doing. Especially when they imagined that by a revolution they were going to bring about conditions where there would not be religion—a 'truly human' society—the same old superstition. They'll maybe have their revolution, they'll spill their rivers of blood, they'll abolish this, that or the other class and the new rulers will hold Marxism up to veneration—because it will be the source of their power over other men. And then gradually men will begin to realize that it is still the same old world, there is still oppression, there is still exploitation, there is still hatred of man by man, until finally some new 'scientific' revolutionary prophet will arise and he'll say, 'Marx and Rousseau and Jefferson and the rest all made revolutions and thought they knew what the result was going to be but, as we know now, it was all ideology. *They* overlooked *this* factor which in the last instance is decisive. *We* recognize *this* factor, so *our* revolution will be different. It will really make men truly human.' And some Saint who has listened to God will be there and, if he weren't so charitable, he would say, 'Lord, what fools these mortals be.'

CHAIRMAN: I must ask you not to pass over into an oration, Streeter. Are there any more specific points you would like to make on the Marxist theory of religion?

STREETER: Yes, very definitely. I am sorry if I let myself become rhetorical. You must understand I feel deeply about all this. All the same, rhetorical or not, what I have been saying is true. However, this is the other point I want to make. I want to deny that religion is the opium of the people, I want to deny that it makes unsatisfactory features of the world acceptable.

I know that religion can be used that way. I know that men who are oppressing others can easily come to believe that God wills it to be so, that it is their sacred duty to go on oppressing and they try to get and succeed in getting the oppressed to believe it is their duty to remain in their oppressed station. That does happen. There is plenty of it in history. You can pervert religion to evil ends but it will be a perverted religion. It happens only insofar as men's eyes are fastened, not on God, but on their worldly interests and in the case of the oppressed, not on God, but on the ideas handed down to them by their social 'superiors'. You remember, 'O, Liberty, what crimes are committed in thy name'. That is perfectly true but it is no disgrace to liberty, it is no responsibility of liberty. Neither is it a disgrace to religion, a responsibility of religion that certain actions are committed in the name of religion. You can fool people about what is the will of God but don't blame that on God, but rather on the worldly interests which lead it to be done and on their worldliness which leads them to be deceived.

Let me make this additional point. Just as there is a so-called religion of acquiescence, so there is a so-called religion of revolt. If you are going to blame (or praise) religion as opium when men stay quiet, you ought also to blame (or praise) religion as stimulant when they revolt. For don't forget that men have revolted in the name of religion. Were the English Puritans of the seventeenth century mere defenders of the status quo? They are only one example. You can supply others for yourselves.

I want to make it quite clear I am not defending the Puritans. I think they were misled as much as the mere acquiescent about the will of God. They got this idea into their heads that they were going to set the world right. They got it from their worldly interests, their secular interests, and then they pinned it on to God as if it was His idea. They took the same arrogant line as the Marxists. Others had been all at sea but this was the real thing. They were God's chosen instruments just as the Marxists imagine themselves to be the instruments of history. And of course it didn't turn out as they expected. It never does. But my main point is that, if you're going to pin acquiescence on religion then don't forget you've got to pin revolt on it too.

Real religion, I would say, is never acquiescent, but neither does it imagine it's going to turn the world upside down by some great machinery changes. It knows that the only real change is a change in the hearts of men, that this is a slow never-ending struggle, that you may help it by improving something social here or something else there. That is the way the really religious work. They do not acquiesce. Religion is no opium for them. It makes them acutely sensitive to injustice, exploitation and all the other hindrances to communion with God. But it makes them also aware that you can't expect mass miracles to which these secular 'scientific' revolutionaries (and some who call themselves religious too) pin their faith.

There, that will do for me, Mr. Chairman. I have talked more than usual tonight, but I could not sit silent and see religion without a defender. I will say no more in this discussion.

CHAIRMAN: Thank you, Streeter. You have certainly raised many issues. I think it would be only fair to give South or Allen a chance to reply, since some of your points are new in the discussion. I will ask them, however, to confine themselves to the new points. Where Streeter was answering points that either South or Allen had already made, I think we had better let the cases rest.

SOUTH: I would like to say something on new points, Mr. Chairman.

1. Even if we accept Streeter's view that God exists, there can be only one set of religious beliefs that is true. All religious beliefs that differ from these true ones must be false. I think that we can certainly explain these false beliefs along the lines Marx follows with the modifications I have suggested.

2. The existence of God. I realize Streeter was very brief here and could give us only an outline of the ways he would demonstrate God's existence. I will also try to be brief.

(a) The so-called working of God in men's lives and the strength that comes from prayer can be explained in psychological and social terms. You can observe the same sort of phenomena when a man becomes really devoted to a purely secular course.

(b) There is no design in nature, there are only things with their own regular ways of working.

(c) We can't accept an experience merely as such. We have to be able to give an account of the nature of the object experienced and that object has to square with the rest of our experience. These 'experiences of God' can be psychologically explained.

3. Much of the rest of Streeter's case breaks down with his demonstration of the existence of God. Indeed, most of it depends directly on that. This applies in particular to the points he labelled 'first', 'second', 'third', 'fourth', 'fifth'.

4. I agree with the point he labelled 'sixth' insofar as it refers to dreams of a 'truly human' society as illusions.

5. I agree too that we find religions of revolt as well as religions of acquiescence.
But I don't want to take up time simply in agreeing, so I'll stop there.

CHAIRMAN: Thank you, South. Now what about you, Allen?

ALLEN: I, too, will be brief.

1. I disagree with both Streeter and South about the possibility of a truly human society. Because Marx points out that previous revolutionaries did not know what they were doing, it does not follow that Marxists do not know what they are doing. Men tried for a long time to transmute metals, even believed they were on the track of doing it. Because they failed for so long, it doesn't mean it can't be done. It now can be done. If Marx thinks the coming revolution will produce a truly human society, it does not follow that he is wrong simply because previous thinkers were wrong about previous revolutions. We have to look into his reasons for thinking this occasion is different. We'll be doing that in a later discussion. Streeter has certainly said nothing to inform us one way or another about whether Marx is right.

2. Streeter is wrong in thinking past revolutions did not achieve anything. They were steps upward, even if not such long steps as participants imagined.

3. About religions of revolt. It is true there are cases like the English Puritans and their religion was their ideology which expressed in an ideological form the class interests which really moved them. By comparison with the old ideology theirs was progressive. But why did they need religion? Because they too were an exploiting class. They stood for an

order more progressive than that of the monarchy and aristocracy they attacked. But, as representatives of commerce, they
had need of opium and there it was in their ideology ready
made for the day when they would be triumphant, when the
austerity, thrift, and diligence which their religion enjoined
would not only help them accumulate capital but also give
them suitable quiescent workers. Because of the pressure of
the productive forces, they revolted but they had their opium
too.

4. It is all very well for Streeter to tell us that religions of
acquiescence were not really religions. That is religion as we
find it on the grand scale in history, as a socially significant
factor. It is not a matter of what he privately chooses to call the
only real religion.

There, Mr. Chairman, I think that will suffice.

VII

Scientific and Utopian Socialism

CHAIRMAN: I thought that in this discussion, gentlemen, we could not do better than look into the distinction which Marx makes between Scientific and Utopian Socialism.

ALLEN: I agree entirely. Anyone who has not grasped the way in which Marx made socialism scientific has missed the distinctive feature of Marx's contribution and the superiority of his theory to the Utopian socialism of his socialist predecessors.

SOUTH: I think Marx is wrong in describing his theory as scientific. I also think he is wrong in some of his criticisms of the Utopians. All the same I think it is important to consider his theories on this point. Even if Marx himself would not have condoned some of the things that have been done in the name of Marxist theory, I think that some of the most despotic of them, some of those which lead furthest away from socialism, insofar as that involves freedom, do get justification from his theories about scientific and Utopian socialism. So on grounds of both theoretical and practical interest I am certainly in favour of taking up this topic.

STREETER: I don't know anything about it but it sounds important. Both Allen who is a Marxist and South who is anti-Marxist agree that it is significant for understanding Marxist theory. That is good enough for me. But I'd like to begin by understanding the terms. I think I have a rough idea of what Marx is likely to mean by scientific socialism.

SOUTH: You'll be surprised.

STREETER: Maybe. Nevertheless I'm content to stand that over for the time being and concentrate on Utopian. I suppose this derives from the name of Sir Thomas More's book *Utopia* in which he describes his ideal society. I suppose that when

Marx describes a socialist as Utopian he means that his socialism doesn't exist, is only an ideal. But of course he must mean
more than that. He must mean also that it couldn't exist. After
all socialism in Marx's own meaning of the word didn't exist
in Marx's own day. Yet he called his own 'scientific' socialism.
He must have meant that one (the 'scientific') could come
about, whereas the other (the 'Utopian') could not come
about. Utopian feet were 'off the ground', if I may put it
colloquially. Is that what Marx meant?

ALLEN: Something like that, only more so. I think, Mr.
Chairman, that these problems of the meaning of 'Utopian'
which are bothering Streeter will become quite clear if I
expound the Marxist view. I can assure Streeter that they
won't be overlooked.

STREETER: That will suit me.

CHAIRMAN: Then I think our best procedure will be to ask
Allen to expound the Marxist position. I think it will be
important, if it is practicable, for you to give us Marx's views
in his own words. That will enable us to check up for ourselves
on his meaning.

ALLEN: I will certainly do that, Mr. Chairman, as I have
done in the past. I will begin by citing a passage written before
Marx was quite clear where he was going. It appeared in the
Franco-German Year Book in 1844. There he wrote

We shall not dogmatically anticipate the coming world, but shall begin by
discovering the new world through criticism of the old one. Hitherto the
philosophers had schemes for the solution of all riddles lying ready in their
desks, and the stupid exoteric world had merely to open its mouth wide that
the roast pigeons of absolute science might fly into its mouth . . . We do not
say to the world: 'Cease your struggles, which are foolish, for we will give
you the true battle-cry.' We merely show the world for what it is really
fighting, and the world must become self-conscious whether it will or no
. . .

And he summarized the aims of the periodical by writing: 'To
make the time fully understand its struggles and its wishes'.

I repeat—this was written while Marx was still young,
before he fully understood his own direction. In this particular
passage there is no special reference to socialism. Nevertheless

he clearly distinguishes between the Utopian approach on the one hand and the scientific approach on the other.

STREETER: Just a moment. Let me get this clear. On the one hand there is the approach which consists of working out in one's head the answer to the world's problems.

ALLEN: Yes. That is the Utopian approach which Marx rejects.

STREETER: Why does he reject it? After all if you don't work out the answers in your head where can you work them out?

ALLEN: I think that question puts it too simply. You will notice that Marx says that the attitude of these scholars is that the rest of the world just has to open its mouth, in other words be receptive to these answers and all will be well. But notice that the rest of the world is referred to as 'stupid'. This implies (I think it is clear from the whole context), both that the world can't work out the answers for itself and also that it won't accept them.

Besides he indicates what these 'philosophers' do by contrast with what he and his friends won't do. 'We shall not dogmatically anticipate the coming world . . .' but these philosophers of whom he speaks do 'dogmatically anticipate the coming world'. They construct theories of what the new world will be like from their own dogmas.

STREETER: You mean from moral dogmas—dogmas about what is good. What ought to be, will be?

ALLEN: Yes that is the kind of thing Marx has in mind. The present order is not just. It would be just if it were arranged in a different way. If men will only accept this just arrangement their problems will be solved. That is one aspect of Utopianism.

STREETER: I see, but one point still troubles me. If this is Utopian and if Marx is contrasting it with science why, when he is describing this approach, does he say that the world had only to open its mouth so that the pigeons of science could fly into its mouth?

ALLEN: He does not say the 'pigeons of science'. He says 'the roast pigeons of absolute science'. His use of 'roast' is important. It implies 'prepared to be eaten', finally ready. But more important for the point you raise, is his use of 'absolute science.' Marx does not believe that this is science. He does not think you get science by working from principles of absolute justice or anything of that kind. For him the scientific approach is the alternative one, the one he himself stands for.

STREETER: I'm not sure that I agree with all that. Perhaps I'll see more clearly if we look at the other side now—this approach which, according to Marx, is scientific. He doesn't dogmatically anticipate the coming world. Instead what was it that he did?

ALLEN: He began with the struggles actually going on in the world.

STREETER: What do you mean by 'he began with them'?

ALLEN: He accepted them. He was prepared to let them be the starting point for his thinking. 'We do not say to the world: "Cease your struggles . . ." we merely show the world for what it is really fighting.'

STREETER: Now I begin to see. This links up with Marx's doctrine of ideologies, with his theory that men don't know what they are struggling about.

ALLEN: Exactly. Here, before Marx, is a struggle going on in the world. He studies it. He says: these are the forces struggling, those are the issues about which they are struggling, and that will be the result. He discovers the new world, the world that will come into being, by studying the world that exists now, not by considering what ought to be. Hence his business is 'to make the world fully understand its struggles and its wishes.' We must remember, as you just said, his view that the world does not fully understand its struggles and its wishes.

STREETER: And why is this scientific and the other approach Utopian?

ALLEN: Surely that is obvious. The scientific method keeps its feet on the ground. It keeps contact with reality. It doesn't spin predictions in its head based on abstract principles but predicts on the basis of existing forces.

STREETER: You mean that a 'solution' which is merely worked out in somebody's head is not a solution because it can't be adopted. It can't possibly arise out of the existing forces in society.

ALLEN: That is correct. It is up in the clouds, Utopian.

STREETER: I think I understand the drift of your argument. But where does the socialism come in?

ALLEN: Not at all in the passage I have quoted. As I said, it is from an early work. Nevertheless once Marx had hit upon the method—the scientific as against the Utopian method—he was bound to see socialism as the answer, as the result of the conflict of the existing forces in society and as the solution of the major social problems. In the very same year as he wrote the passage I have given you, Marx wrote the major part of *The Holy Family* and in this he is quite explicit. He argues that private property is compelled to maintain the existence of the proletariat, that it is compelled to dehumanize this proletariat which is therefore compelled to revolt and abolish itself (i.e. as proletariat) and therefore to abolish private property. He writes,

We are not concerned with what this or that proletarian or the proletariat as a whole, may regard as an aim. What we are concerned with is what the proletariat actually is; and what the proletariat will, in accordance with the nature of its own being, be historically compelled to do. Its goal and its historical action are obvious, are irrevocably indicated, in the vital situation of the proletariat, and also in the whole organisation of contemporary bourgeois society.

STREETER: I can see that he is stressing there that certain action will be forced on the proletariat and that it will have certain results. But does he give any reasons for thinking that the proletariat will play this role in history?

ALLEN: Yes, he does. I have already summarized his reasons, but here they are in his own words:

When Socialist writers ascribe this role in universal history they are far from doing so because they regard proletarians as gods. It is very much the other way. Because, in the fully developed proletariat, the withdrawal of all humanity, and even of the semblance of humanity, has been practically completed; because, in the living conditions of the proletariat, all the living conditions of contemporary society are comprised in their unhuman climax; because in the proletariat, the human being has lost himself; but has gained something more than the theoretical awareness of this loss, for he has gained this in addition, that it has become an imperious necessity for him to revolt against inhumanity—for all these reasons, the proletariat can and must liberate itself.

STREETER: Are these the only reasons he gives?

ALLEN: They are sufficient surely. However, in the course of his life's work he was to point out how capitalism must become a fetter upon productive forces, how it must break down, how it must organize workers on a large scale in factories, how this must give them the opportunity and the impetus to organize themselves in Trades Unions and politically, how the struggle against oppression must itself gradually teach them their own power (due to both numbers and their key position in production), and the full scope of the task before them. However all this secured full elaboration only with time. I think Otto Rühle, the biographer of Marx, sums up very well the point which is essential for our present discussion. Writing of *The Holy Family*, he says:

> What the utopists had never grasped, namely that socialism must be the outcome of a historical evolution, and that this evolution must be brought to pass by a self-conscious and independent movement on the part of the working class, secured lucid and cogent expression for the first time.

STREETER: But did Marx himself never say it?

ALLEN: Yes he did. For example only a couple of years later, in *The German Ideology*, he wrote:

> For us communism is not a condition of affairs which 'ought' to be established, not an 'ideal' towards which reality has to direct itself. When we speak of communism, we mean the actual movement which makes an end of the present condition of affairs.

STREETER: That certainly seems to confirm your interpretation of his meaning.

ALLEN: I don't think there is any doubt about my interpretation. In the same work he makes another point—'Not criticism, but revolution, is the motive force of history'. You can see how, for the Utopians, the propounding of their ideas and getting them accepted would be the essential thing. Hence criticism, not revolution, would be the motive force of history. But for Marx 'consciousness does not determine life, but life determines consciousness'. If we take this in conjunction with the fact to which he also drew attention, namely that no ruling class surrenders power voluntarily, you can see why he would say 'not criticism but revolution'.

STREETER: And for the society of his own day it would be the socialist revolution.

ALLEN: Exactly. In his full maturity Marx hammered away at the distinction between scientific and Utopian socialism. In 1871 in *The Civil War in France*, he wrote:

The working class did not expect miracles from the (Paris) Commune. They have no ready-made utopias to introduce by popular decree. They know that in order to work out their own emancipations and along with it that higher form to which present society is irresistibly tending, by its own economical agencies, they will have to pass through long struggles, through a series of historic processes, transforming circumstances and men. They have no ideals to realise, but to set free the elements of the new society . . .

You see the same line of thought—no ready-made Utopias, no ideals, but instead setting free elements of the new society already in the old, an irresistible course of historical development.

CHAIRMAN: Is that all, Allen?

ALLEN: It is far from all, Mr. Chairman, but I'm afraid that it is all with which we can hope to deal in the time at our disposal. I should like merely to add certain reminders—firstly, that this irresistible development of history is dialectical, secondly, that Marx undertook monumental economic studies in which he demonstrated that capitalism must collapse, thirdly, that the materialist conception of history indicates the way in which history follows its inevitable path to socialism. That will satisfy me for the present, Mr. Chairman, though I may find it necessary to seek your permission to say some more when I hear some of South's criticisms—though how South can espouse the cause of the Utopians against Scientific Socialism I am at a loss to conceive.

SOUTH: That is because you forget that it is not necessary to defend the Utopians in order to assert that Marx's socialism is not scientific.

CHAIRMAN: Just a moment, South. Let me first attempt to summarize the Marxist position as Allen has expounded it. These are the main points as I understood them:

1. The Utopians constructed ideal societies in their heads.

2. They believed that if men would accept their ideals they would solve their social problems.

3. They were moved by such conceptions as 'justice' or other moral principles or something similar.

Would that do as a very brief summary of the Utopians, Allen?

ALLEN: Yes, that would do. Perhaps I should add that Marx did not deny that the work of the Utopians had some value in exposing some features of existing society.

CHAIRMAN: Very well, we will note that. Nevertheless he criticized them severely from the point of view of Scientific socialism. His main arguments were—

1. History was bound to follow certain paths so it was pointless to conceive ideal societies.

2. The important thing was to study the actual movement of history.

3. This study revealed that history was moving in the direction of socialism.

4. Socialism by abolishing private property would solve the main problems of contemporary society.

5. It is not a question, then, of moral principles or of feelings of hatred or love or compassion but rather of scientific demonstration.

Will that do, Allen?

ALLEN: That is correct as far as it goes, Mr. Chairman, but don't forget the arguments about the course of history and the role of the proletariat.

CHAIRMAN: I have not forgotten those. South may refer to them if he wishes but I did not summarize them because we have either already discussed them or we shall do so in the near future. Now South.

SOUTH: Well, Mr. Chairman, I have so much to say that I hardly know where to begin.

STREETER: I gather then, that in this matter you seriously disagree with Marx.

SOUTH: I do. His description of his socialism as 'scientific' has had important propaganda effects. It has given his followers a feeling of having their feet on the ground and a certainty and a contempt for alternative positions which may very well have been valuable in helping them to do *something*, but which is certainly not scientific in spirit. And I believe this is due to the fact that in its main features Marx's position is not scientific at all but rather religious and Utopian.

STREETER: You mean you reject his position lock, stock and barrel.

SOUTH: No, things are rarely so simple that it is possible to do that. There are some points in his theory that are sound, that do mark a scientific approach.

STREETER: Such as—?

SOUTH: Such as his insistence that if you are predicting what is going to happen, then you cannot do it in terms of what ought to be. You can do it only by studying existing forces.

STREETER: I'm not sure.

SOUTH: It is true, no doubt that men often forget it when they are dealing with particular issues. They say: 'I believe there will be one world government. There will have to be or men will destroy themselves with their modern weapons.'

STREETER: Quite so.

SOUTH: Well, that is just plain Utopianism. The fact that you can see only two alternatives, one of which you don't like, is not a sufficient reason for believing that the one you prefer will happen. If you are going to establish that it will happen, you have to do it in a different way—by showing that it is the upshot of the existing forces.

STREETER: That is exactly what Marx says.

SOUTH: I know that. I am giving you, first of all, my points of agreement with Marx. I have a second point of agreement—another aspect of Marx's determinism. You remember that Allen quoted for us the famous passage about the proletariat. It isn't a question of what this or that proletarian, or even the proletariat as a whole, at any given time thinks, it is a question of what the proletariat will be compelled to do in view of its nature and position in society. I agree with that sort of approach. We could say the same about any other section of society. Determinism is a necessary part of any scientific approach.

STREETER: If you are prepared to go as far as this with Marx, haven't you given your whole case away.

SOUTH: Not by any means. There is nothing distinctively

Marxist about predicting only on the basis of existing forces and recognizing that forces act in accordance with their character and environment. These two things simply mean determinism. Once we accept that all things have causes and effects we have to accept them. But there is nothing distinctively Marxist about that. Many non-Marxists would accept it.

STREETER: I wouldn't, but still go on.

CHAIRMAN: You wouldn't accept it, Streeter? Then we had better have your views later on.

STREETER: I'll be glad to give them. I have the feeling all along that South's criticism of Marx is too namby-pamby. He gives too much away.

SOUTH: Not at all, Streeter. I must concede that Marx is right on the points where he is right. Besides, don't forget this: Marxists have gained a superior sense of being scientific and a contempt for their critics just because some of their critics have attacked them on the very points where their position is sound, is scientific. They have no difficulty in defending these points and then imagine that the religious and Utopian features of their system are similarly defensible and scientific. If a criticism of Marxism is to be sound it must draw a clear line between what is scientific in Marxism and what is not.

STREETER: I don't agree with you about these so-called scientific features, but still get on with the business. Where do you think Marx goes off the rails?

SOUTH: In a number of places. Perhaps a good place to start would be on a point which Allen did not make, probably because he takes it so much for granted. Marx was claiming to be not only a theorist about politics but also a practitioner, not merely a politicist but also a politician, not merely a critic but also a revolutionary. Indeed the two sides—theory and practice—were for him part of one and the same activity.

STREETER: Yes, we saw that in an early discussion, but where does it lead us now?

SOUTH: It leads us to this point. When Marx regards his socialism as scientific, he is thinking of more than this: that it is a theory that out of the existing facts will come Socialism. He means that it can be scientifically demonstrated that the existing forces will produce socialism. But he means more than that. He means as well that here is a reason for action. You should be a Socialist because that is what is going to happen. And he imagines that this is a scientific motivation whereas the Utopian approach—let us say for example, 'You should be a socialist because socialism would be more just than the present order'—such an approach is, according to him, unscientific.

STREETER: I believe you're on the track of something important there. I'd like to hear you develop it at length.

SOUTH: I think it is important. Marx scoffed at such motivation as 'justice'. He believed that this was a sentimental approach. Now I am not saying that he was entirely wrong in his criticism of the Utopians. Insofar as they thought that in the principle of justice—however it is worked out in detail—they had something to command universal acceptance; they were wrong. Men are for or against justice according to their interests. If you can demonstrate that a certain state of affairs is just, you do *not* thereby supply a motive for all men to try to create that state of affairs. It is a motive only for those who agree with your conception of justice and who support it. Some will be for it, some against it, according to what they are, according to their natures. The more they understand it, the more some people will be against it, because they will see clearly that it harms their interests. So insofar as Utopians imagined that it was merely necessary to demonstrate that socialism was more just than the existing state of society, in order to bring it about, they were wrong. Their demonstrations could appeal only to those who supported their conception of justice.

But Marx is in no better position. He is trying to escape from this limited appeal of the Utopians as well as from their lack of realism. He is trying to show that the very nature of things requires men to be socialists and he believes that his demonstration of this is scientific. You are Utopian if you struggle for Socialism because you believe it to be just and you want justice, but you are scientific if you support socialism because you believe it is going to happen.

Now I say that the first kind of motivation is the only kind you can get. You cannot get away from men's wants in the matter of motivation—a point which Marx himself recognized in other connections. You cannot get a scientific motivation: You can find the facts to be so and so but the facts in themselves do not tell you what to do. You can find out what to do only if you consider the facts in relation to your wants. Thus Streeter and I may each recognize the same set of facts and yet each be impelled to different action by them because our demands are different.

So even if we grant all of Marx's arguments about what is going to happen, even if we grant that he has demonstrated to our entire satisfaction that Socialism will come about, this is not a motivation for being a socialist unless we want to be on the side of what is going to happen. It does not provide a scientific basis for socialism as Marx thought it did. We might believe Marx's predictions and still fight against socialism.

ALLEN: I am sorry to interrupt, Mr. Chairman, but I feel that I must. South's case seems to me so patently unsound that he ought not to be allowed to get away with it. If he believes that socialism is inevitable and yet he fights against it, surely he is being unscientific. Of course he may choose to make a martyr of himself for a lost cause but that is not really fighting for it. It is merely satisfying a personal need. Really fighting for a cause means taking steps towards its victory. If you don't believe it can be victorious—and, indeed, whatever you believe, if the fact is that it can't be victorious—then there are no steps towards its victory. If you try to take them you may be quixotic but you certainly can't be scientific. You are out of touch with reality.

SOUTH: Allen's argument is thoroughly unsound, though I admit that it is consistent with Marxism. Indeed it underlines some of the central weaknesses of Marxism which I have already pointed out in earlier dicussions. It rests on the assumption that there is one track in history—from slave society, through feudalism and capitalism to socialism, a single track because all other spheres of social life are mere expressions of the economic structure. If you accept that theory, then it would certainly be true that your fight against socialism would be futile. But even that would not necessarily mean that there was anything unscientific about it. You might be just as much in touch with reality as people on the winning side. You might say, 'I know I am going to lose but still I would rather go down fighting than submit to a socialist society.' There is nothing unscientific about that. Fighting is not simply taking steps towards winning. It is taking steps in opposition to another force. Whether we would judge it to be futile would depend once again on our demands. If we demand that anything we fight for must win then it would be futile (on the Marxist assumptions). But if we demand that we fight for what we believe in, for what we support, then it would not be futile. You can't get away from demands. It is no good trying to escape from them by pretending that your motivation is purely scientific. Motivation cannot be purely scientific, i.e. dictated entirely by the facts of the case, because the facts of the case cannot tell you what to do. Even the fact that one side is inevitably going to win cannot tell you to get on to that side. That too, is partly a matter of your demands.

And all this, Mr. Chairman, is on the Marxist assumption of historical monism, of a single track in history. As you know I reject that assumption. I have given my reasons in earlier discussions. Even if we can say that there are economic systems and even if we can classify them broadly as slave, feudal, capitalist and socialist, or in some other way, and even if we can say that in the economic field one of these systems is, at a given time dominant, nevertheless it is not the only system in existence. There is a plurality of economic systems, intermingled, even if some are less important in the broad picture than others. Besides I have refuted the view that the rest of social history is a mere expression of the economic. It has its history, or more exactly many histories. I stand for the view that society is a plurality of forces. There is art, for example, with its many schools—not all mere expressions of the economic structure.

CHAIRMAN: Yes, yes, we have heard you argue all this before and some of us may agree with you, but will you please come to its application to the present case.

SOUTH: Certainly I will. It applies very directly. If society is a plurality and even if Socialism is inevitable, then this means that socialism becomes dominant in the economic sphere and has a powerful influence on other spheres. But it does not mean that other economic systems will disappear entirely. It does not mean that in politics, science, art, social customs and so on, only those activities will survive which are supported by socialism. Other activities will survive. They may be stronger or weaker. It is not a case of all black or all white. Even if it can be shown that socialism is going to triumph, this can only mean that it is going to become dominant and its dominance is a matter of degree. The degree of its dominance will be affected by the vigour with which its opponents resist it and its supporters support it. The opponent of socialism who recognizes that is being quite scientific. On the other hand Marx in imagining that the existing forces are going to lead to a society which can be adequately characterized as socialist is being Utopian. You never get societies which can be characterized in a blanket way like that.

STREETER: You mean that we can't describe our society as capitalist?

SOUTH: Yes, I mean that 'capitalist' is not an adequate description of any society. It may serve as a shorthand way of indicating that capitalism is very strong in the society, but if we use it to characterize the society we ignore the fact that it is not even an adequate description of the economic structure, let alone the political, religious, scientific or artistic features of the society. It is simply fantastic that anyone aware of the complexities of society could take this kind of blanket description seriously. Of course Marx makes it sound plausible by his monist conception of society but this itself won't stand examination. His socialism is not scientific but Utopian.

STREETER: You said that it was religious too. Why do you say that?

SOUTH: Because he believes that there is a single path of historical development and that history is fighting on the side of the socialists who will therefore win in the end. History in this sense—this single track sense—doesn't exist. It is a supernatural entity. Surely this is a religious doctrine of the predestination kind. I won't elaborate this argument. You can read it for yourself in Max Eastman's book, Marxism—Is it Science?

STREETER: I certainly will, and I'll have to think about your argument. I suppose you'd say that this is where Marxism gets its appeal.

SOUTH: Of course that is where it gets its appeal. It is a religious doctrine and God (or History) is on the side of the Socialists and is bound to make them win in the end. It does all the things many religions do—promises a rosy future, gives consolation for temporary set-backs, gives assurance of a super-personal support in the difficulties of struggle, gives an enemy who does damage now but nevertheless will eventually and inevitably be overthrown, and simplifies all struggles down ultimately to one struggle. All the talk about putting socialism on a scientific basis won't stand examination.

STREETER: Well, you certainly aren't pulling any punches tonight. Yet I gather you agree with Marx that socialism will be victorious although you say that this is a matter of degree.

SOUTH: I do not agree. I do not think he has done more than begin to make his case. He argues that capitalism will come to an end. We have hardly the time to look into that in detail but let us grant him the point. Assume that capitalism will collapse. What follows? It certainly does not follow that socialism will succeed it. Many possibilities have to be left open. It still has to be argued that the workers will take control and run society. And what arguments has he for that? He tells us that capitalism dehumanizes the workers and forces them to revolt. I question whether it dehumanizes as much as he thinks. I further question whether it is dehumanization which forces revolt. But even if it be assumed to be so, how far have we got? We would simply have established on these very doubtful assumptions that the workers will revolt. But that gets us no nearer our goal. The workers could revolt in support of a new set of rulers who denounced the old set of rulers and clamped down their own rule, their own exploitation on the workers. We have seen this sort of thing happen before. Slaves have revolted, serfs have revolted. Have these revolts meant slave or serf rulers or a society of common property, or of freedom and equality? The mere fact of revolt indicates a certain amount of enterprise. It does not necessarily indicate sufficient enterprise to run society, much less to undertake the far more difficult task of running a co-operative society. It is true that the workers combine, organize, and become a significant political factor in society. We have seen that happen. But that does not establish that they can do what Marx expected them to do. Before he leaped to that conclusion he needed to examine the existing forces much more closely, to look carefully at the nature of the workers' movement and at the nature of the competing movements. Of course he was precluded from doing that by the over-simplification that the struggle was becoming more and more capitalists on one side, workers on the other. Hence if the capitalists went down, the workers would have to go up. There was and is no more reason for saying that, than for saying that if the feudal lords went down the serfs would run a classless society. To predict the outcome of present social struggles we have to examine a complexity of social forces weighing up the strength and potentialities of each. Marx certainly hasn't done the job. From a scientific point of view his method is quite unsound. It is not scientific socialism.

CHAIRMAN: Unless you have some really vital point to make, South, I must ask you to stop. I think you have said sufficient to indicate the line of your thought. I want to give Streeter a very brief time to state where he disagrees with you and Allen. Will you be as brief as you can be, Streeter?

STREETER: I'll do my best. I cannot accept the position taken up by Marx and agreed to by both Allen and South, that a scientific method in social science means determinism. After all we are dealing here with human beings and there is the human will. If men resolve to make a better order of society they can make it. Not a perfect world of course. I stated the limits to what they can do in a previous discussion. Nevertheless the only way to get a better world is if men will it to be so. Whether a socialist world would be better is another question. I disagree with the Utopians insofar as they thought they would get a Utopia. I agree with South that Marx was a Utopian who wouldn't do more than sketch his Utopia. But I agree with the Utopians insofar as they were making a moral appeal to men. Men were free to choose. The evil in their hearts would mean that you would never get a perfect world. But to choose good, not evil, was and is the path upward.

VIII
The Workers under Capitalism

CHAIRMAN: I have been considering what aspect of Marxism we ought to discuss next. We have only two more meetings after this one and that means obviously that there are many aspects of Marx's political doctrine that we must leave untouched. So I think we should concentrate on something which is of central importance.

ALLEN: I agree entirely, and I feel that there is one aspect to which we have not yet given anywhere near adequate attention, and that is the role of the workers.

SOUTH: Hear! Hear! Marx assigns to them such a major part in the politics of our age that we must consider his theories about them.

STREETER: I'm happy about that, but there is another matter I want to hear something about too and that is the Communist Party.

CHAIRMAN: Very well. That gives us a programme for our last three discussions. Tonight we'll consider the workers before the revolution.

ALLEN: The workers under capitalism.

CHAIRMAN: Yes. Then at our next meeting we'll consider the workers and their part after the revolution.

ALLEN: The Dictatorship of the Proletariat.

CHAIRMAN: Yes, we can call it that. Then finally we will discuss the Task of the Communists.

SOUTH: You mean Marx's theory of the Task of the Communists.

CHAIRMAN: Yes, Marx's theory. Are we all agreed? We are? Good. Then, Allen, will you please outline Marx's theory of the Workers under Capitalism?

ALLEN: With pleasure, Mr. Chairman. I'd like to point out

firstly, though, that on all these topics which we have still to discuss, a great deal of confusion exists. The Russian Communists, who call themselves Marxists, succeeded in securing control of a great state after a revolution. Naturally this fact greatly increased the prestige of their theories. In particular, their claim that their theories were Marxist came to be widely believed, except among those who were prepared to examine the position carefully. Yet the claims of the Russian Communists are far from the truth. Certainly there are important Marxist aspects in their theories, but there are also very important respects in which they depart seriously from Marxism, and nowhere is this difference deeper than in the theories of the role of the workers and of the Communists. I mention this because I know that many who read the report of our discussion will feel that the theory I am expounding is not Marxist because it disagrees with the exposition of Lenin, who is also claiming to be Marxist. I want to make it quite clear that what I am expounding is Marx's Marxism and that Lenin's is not.

CHAIRMAN: You are quite entitled, in a case like this, where there is a dispute among people calling themselves Marxist, about what Marxism really is—you are quite entitled to cite these other people such as Lenin, and to try to show on the basis of quotations how they diverge from Marxism.

ALLEN: I'm glad of that, Mr. Chairman. I was afraid you might regard such a discussion as a digression.

CHAIRMAN: Not at all. It may even help to bring out the real meaning of Marx if we consider alternative interpretations.

ALLEN: Good. Then I'll go right ahead. I think I should begin by a quotation which we have noticed several times already:

> It is not a question of what this or that Proletarian, or even the Proletariat as a whole, may imagine for the moment to be the aim. It is a question of what the proletariat actually is and what it will be compelled to do historically as the result of this being. The aim and the Historical action of the proletariat are laid down in advance, irrevocably and obviously, in its own situation in life and in the whole organisation of contemporary bourgeois society.

STREETER: Yes, we've considered that before. The workers' action will be determined by what they are and by their place in society. But, even if we accept that, it does not get us very far. We need to know what they are and what is their position in society. Otherwise we cannot tell what they will do.

ALLEN: Quite so. In our last discussion we saw part of Marx's answer to these questions. In bourgeois society the proletariat is dehumanized, 'It does not suffer one specific injustice, but . . . . . injustice unqualified', it 'has been completely deprived of its human privileges.' This dehumanization of the proletariat, this complete deprivation of human privileges makes it 'an imperious necessity for him to revolt against inhumanity'.

STREETER: Yes, and you also told us that this revolt was helped by the breakdown of capitalism itself, by the fact that capitalism was forced to organize the workers in factories, thereby making it possible for them to organize themselves in unions and political parties, and that they would learn in the course of their struggles. I made a note of all that.

ALLEN: Correct. That point about learning in the course of the struggle is particularly important. Workers had to go through long struggles 'not merely in order to change conditions, but to change [themselves] and make themselves fit to take over political power'. And then there is the equally important development in Marx's theory—the revolt of the workers will be such that it will emancipate not merely themselves, not merely the workers but the whole of society.

STREETER: What is his reason for saying that?

ALLEN: The very fact that the proletariat is completely without privileges. If it had some privileges, then when it made its revolution it would be satisfied with a state of affairs that gave a satisfactory life to those with these privileges. Any who did not have the privileges would not be emancipated from dehumanization by such a revolution. The bourgeois revolution was of this kind. There is no doubt that under feudalism or an aristocratic regime the bourgeoisie suffered certain disabilities. They were not, for example, politically enfranchised. The right to play a part in ruling the country was a privilege of birth. Certain offices were not open to them. The right to build their own churches in which they could worship in their own way was not open to them. They were subject to sundry tolls, levies, and obstructions on their trade by the aristocracy. And so on. From grievances like these arose their tendency to revolt. And when they revolted, they sought emancipation and secured it. But it was not an emancipation for everyone in society. Some were left as dehumanized as before, and the reason was that the bourgeoisie even in the old society already possessed important privileges. They had the ownership of means of production and this ownership carried with it the ability to do other things, for example, provide the leisure for their children to be educated, publish their views and thereby organize political and other support, fight costly law cases and so on. They had plenty of interest in abolishing the special privileges of the aristocracy—at least so far as such special privileges interfered with them—but they certainly did not have an interest in abolishing their own special privileges nor in any social changes which conferred a satisfactory life on those who did not enjoy their privileges. They were quite happy to say that every man was equal before the law, but they were equally happy to forbear from looking into the question of how far the worker could in fact, let us say, carry an appeal to the Privy Council. Certainly he had a right to do it just as they had. They could do it. They had the money and the education. But whatever rights he had, could he, in fact, exercise them? Could he, in fact, afford to give his children a University education, even if he had a right to do so? Could he, in fact, publish his opinions, even if he had a right to do so? The bourgeoisie established conditions which emancipated people in the same position as the bourgeoisie, people who had their privileges, but it did not emancipate the whole of society because a large part of society did not have these privileges.

STREETER: I see that, and you are saying that because the workers have no special privileges (such as the bourgeoisie has), the workers can emancipate themselves only by creating conditions which will mean the emancipation of all?

ALLEN: Exactly.

CHAIRMAN: That is very interesting, Allen, and you say that it is Marx's view. Don't you think that you had better support that by telling us exactly what Marx has to say about it?

ALLEN: Certainly, Mr. Chairman, I had intended to do

that. In *The Holy Family* Marx says that the proletariat 'cannot liberate itself without abolishing its own living conditions, without abolishing all the unhuman living conditions of contemporary society, the conditions that comprise the situation of the proletariat'. In *German Ideology* he says that

a class is evolved which has to bear all the burdens of society without enjoying its advantages, which is forced out of society into the most marked contrast to all other classes; a class which forms the majority of all the members of society, and one from which the consciousness of the necessity for a thorough going revolution, the communist consciousness, proceeds. . . .

And further, in the same work,

In all revolutions that have hitherto taken place, the kind of activity has remained inviolate, so that there has never been anything more than a changed distribution of this activity, with a new distribution of labour to other persons: whereas the communist revolution is directed against the kind of activity which has hitherto been exercised, and does away with labour, and makes an end of class rule when it does away with classes, the reason being that this revolution is brought about by the class which no longer counts in society as a class, is not recognised as a class, but is the expression of the dissolution of all classes, nationalities, etc., within extant society. For the widespread generation of this communist consciousness, and for the carrying out of the communist revolution, an extensive change in human beings is needed, which can only occur in the course of a practical movement, in the course of a revolution; so that the revolution is not only necessary because the ruling class cannot be overthrown in any other way, but is also necessary because only in a revolution can the uprising class free itself from the old yoke and become capable of founding a new society.

I will give only one more quotation on this aspect of Marxism. It is from Marx's *Introduction to a Critique of the Hegelian Philosophy of Right*. There Marx poses the question: 'Upon what does a partial, an exclusively political revolution rest?' and he answers,

Upon this, that a particular class, from a position peculiar to itself, should undertake to effect the general emancipation of society. That class can free the whole of society, but only on the proviso that the whole of society is in the position of that class.

STREETER: It certainly seems that Marx's position is as you stated it.

CHAIRMAN: Is there anything else that Marx has to say about the workers under capitalism?

ALLEN: Yes, Mr. Chairman, there is much more, but I think I will concentrate on one particular aspect, partly because it is important in itself, partly because it has been the subject of much misunderstanding in our own day and the real Marxist position has been obscured largely through the influence of Lenin and his followers. In the first article of the Statutes of the First International, Marx wrote that 'The emancipation of the working class must be the act of the workers themselves,' and we have already seen that he thought it would take a long time for the workers to fit themselves to take over political power.

STREETER: Well, what is the special difficulty about that?

ALLEN: It is not a question of difficulty. I think the interpretation is perfectly plain, but it has been challenged in the name of Marxism. Marx and Engels thought of history becoming conscious of itself, in other words, that the people making history in the Communist Revolution know what they are doing, whereas, in previous revolutions they had not done so. In 1895, in his Preface to Marx's *Class Struggles in France*, Engels wrote:

The epoch of violent uprisings, of revolutions carried out by small minorities at the head of unenlightened masses, is past. Where it is a question of the complete transformation of the social organism the masses themselves must take a conscious part in the game, and understand the issues at stake, and the cause for which they are fighting. We have learned this from the history of the last fifty years. However, in order that the masses shall understand what they have to do, long and patient work is necessary, and it is to this work that we are now addressing ourselves with a success which is driving our enemies to despair.

STREETER: To whom does he refer when he says 'we'?

ALLEN: He means the parties of the Second International. But that is not the crucial point now.

CHAIRMAN: We'll probably be going into that when we discuss the task of the Communists.

ALLEN: Quite so. What we have to consider now is Engels' assertion that 'the masses themselves must take a concsious part in the game'. They must understand what they are doing, why they are doing it, and where it will lead. This will be history conscious of itself. It means that the workers considered as individuals or considered in their organizations will understand the situation and the decisions—in other words, they will be *their* decisions. Only in this way will they be free. 'Free Will', says Engels in *Anti-Dühring*, 'is nothing but the capacity to come to a decision in full knowledge of all the facts', and it consists in 'that sovereignty over ourselves and over the outside world founded upon a knowledge of the essential laws of nature', which of course includes the laws of social development. I think the meaning of all this is perfectly clear. Not only does it emerge from the quotations themselves, it is also plain from the facts of the case. The Socialist revolution will be the emancipation of the working class. Therefore the workers must, and will, make this revolution themselves freely, in full knowledge of what they are doing, collectively determining policy. In other words, the workers must and will be democratically organized. They will have discipline but it will be the self-imposed discipline of men joined together freely in joint actions in a common cause widely understood.

STREETER: I can see that that makes sense. It hangs together. But it all rests on the assumption that there is going to be a socialist revolution which is the emancipation of the workers.

ALLEN: That is not an assumption at all. In our earlier discussions I showed how Marxism proved it.

CHAIRMAN: We had better not go over that ground again but merely note that that issue is relevant here.

ALLEN: Very well, Mr. Chairman. The main point I am trying to make is that Marxism conceived the workers' movement as a democratic movement making its decisions collectively by widespread discussion on the basis of widespread enlightenment.

STREETER: But the Marxist parties I know are not like that. They are highly centralized and tightly disciplined—I mean in a military sense of discipline, not in that spontaneous sense you were talking about.

ALLEN: Exactly. That is precisely the point I was coming to, and the main thing I want to say about it is that these are not Marxist Parties. They are Leninist. It is true that Lenin claimed to be Marxist but, especially on this point, he was not. It is significant that he carried not one leading Marxist thinker with him on these questions of organization. The other leading Russian Marxists repudiated him on these questions as un-Marxist. Martov, Axelrod, Trotsky (though Trotsky was converted in 1917), Plekhanov attacked him on the issue, though admittedly some were shaky at times. The great European Marxists, like Kautsky and Luxemburg, also attacked him. I think we get a clear conception of the difference from one passage by Lenin and a reply by Luxemburg. Lenin wrote in *One Step Forward, Two Steps Back*:

'Practical Worker' . . . denounces me for visualising the Party as 'an immense factory' with a director in the shape of the C.C. at its head. . . . 'Practical Worker' does not realise that the frightful word he utters immediately betrays the mentality of a bourgeois intellectual who is familiar with neither the practice nor the theory of proletarian organisation. For it is precisely the factory, which some seem to regard as a bogey, that is the highest form of capitalist co-operation which has brought together and disciplined the proletariat, taught it to organise and placed it at the head of all other sections of the toiling and exploited population. It is precisely Marxism, as the ideology of the proletariat trained by capitalism, that has been teaching unstable intellectuals to distinguish between the factory as an instrument of exploitation (discipline based on the fear of starvation) and as a factor in organisation (discipline based on collective work, united under conditions of technically highly developed production). The discipline and organisation, which is so difficult for the bourgeois intellectual to acquire, are easily acquired by the proletarian precisely because of the factory 'school' he goes through. Mortal fear of this school and complete inability to understand its importance as an organising force are characteristic of ways of thinking which reflect a petty-bourgeois mode of life.

STREETER: And what did Luxemburg have to say to that?
ALLEN: She wrote in reply:

The discipline which Lenin means is impressed upon the proletariat not only by the factory, but also by the barracks and by modern bureaucratism, in short, by the entire mechanism of the centralised bourgeois state. But it is nothing less than the abuse of a general term, which at the same time designates as discipline two such opposing concepts as the wilfulness and the thoughtlessness of a many-limbed, many-armed mass of flesh carrying out mechanical movements at the beat of the baton, and the voluntary co-ordination of the conscious political action of a social stratum; the corpselike obedience of a dominated class and the organised rebellion of a class struggling for freedom. It is not by making use of the discipline impressed upon him by the capitalist state, with a mere transfer of the baton from the hand of the bourgeoisie to that of a Social Democratic Central Committee, but it is only by breaking through and uprooting this slavish spirit of discipline that the proletariat can be educated for a new discipline: the voluntary self-discipline of Social Democracy.

STREETER: And yet Lenin succeeded where the others failed. Even if it is true that he was not Marxist—and I am prepared to grant you that—doesn't this simply show that Marx and all the others including Luxemburg were wrong?

ALLEN: No, it certainly does not. Lenin succeeded in securing state power for himself and for his party, but he did not succeed in making the Socialist revolution, in the emancipation of the workers and of the whole of society, and that was what the Marxists were interested in.

STREETER: But, surely that is not a fair criticism. We can't forget that Russia was a backward country.

ALLEN: That is precisely the point. Russia was a backward country. Its workers and its forces of production were immature, and for just that reason the socialist revolution was impossible there at that time. That is what all the Marxists pointed out. Lenin wanted to take a short cut. The workers were immature, so let them obey his party. He deluded himself that this was or would lead to the emancipation of the workers, whereas, in fact, it gave them a new oppression. Everything that has happened since confirms how wrong he was, and how right were his Marxist critics.

CHAIRMAN: There you are raising a big question about which there are different opinions. You say that the history of Russia—or the Soviet Union as it is now called—shows that Lenin was wrong. There is a school of thought which holds that the subsequent history of Russia shows that he was right. I am afraid that the discussion of that question would lead us off our main track. We'll have to be satisfied with merely posing the issue.

ALLEN: I'm content with that, Mr. Chairman, more particularly as I think that anyone who weighs up the quotations I have given cannot fail to see, from the facts of the case, that Luxemburg is right and Lenin is wrong, and, apart from that, that Luxemburg is a Marxist and Lenin is not.

CHAIRMAN: I must ask you then to bring your exposition to an end unless there is something Streeter wants to ask about.

STREETER: As a matter of fact, there is, Mr. Chairman. Doesn't Marx say that under capitalism the ranks of the workers are increased and their condition worsened?

CHAIRMAN: Be concise, Allen.

ALLEN: I will. Yes, Marx says that. Intermediate classes are gradually eliminated, for example many petty bourgeoisie are driven out of business and become workers, so that we find society more and more lined up in two opposing camps—capitalists and workers. And it is also true that the condition of the workers worsens until they are compelled to rebel. Marx supports this with various arguments. Do you want me to expound them, Mr. Chairman?

CHAIRMAN: No, I think not, Allen. We have to allow time for opposing views. Perhaps if any of the criticism bears directly on these points and we feel it is necessary, then you can do so.

STREETER: I want to challenge Allen's last assertion, Mr. Chairman. It seems to me obviously false. If you look at the last hundred years you must agree that the conditions of the workers have improved. Hours of work have shortened, real wages have risen, safety devices have been installed, in general conditions of work have become better. I needn't go into such matters as child labour, rights to organize, right to holidays and many other things. I'm not disputing that Marx said that the workers' conditions would worsen, and I'm not doubting that he supported this conclusion with many learned arguments. But I am saying that he was wrong.

CHAIRMAN: I want to avoid if I can another long exposition of the Marxist position; nevertheless, I think I should give Allen the opportunity to answer that if you don't mind, South.

SOUTH: I don't mind.

CHAIRMAN: Go ahead, Allen.

ALLEN: Streeter is overlooking this fact—the workers have

been struggling now for a long time. Such improvements as have been brought about in some countries—and I stress 'some'—are due to this struggle. Emancipation is not something that is not here today and here tomorrow. It can be a gradual thing, even if it does involve a violent revolution. What Marx argued was that it was the tendency of capitalism to depress workers' conditions, whereas the tendency of the workers' struggle was to elevate them. However, despite the workers' struggle, there have been terrible worsenings of conditions directly attributable to capitalism in its death agonies. Can Streeter so easily forget that in the last half century we have seen a great depression and the two most terrible wars in history? He can't ignore the burdens the workers have had to carry in those times, as unemployed, as cannon fodder, as displaced persons, as inmates of concentration camps, the millions and millions starved, shot, enslaved, driven mad—I need not detail the horrors of the last half century. It is one of the most terrible times in history. Can Streeter really feel sure that Marx was wrong? There is another approach too. Marx looked not at this country or at that, but at the world. Capitalism created the world market. It is true that the capitalists of some Western countries were able to keep their own workers comparatively quiet by exploiting colonies or semi-colonies and letting the workers at home share the booty. If we are considering the workers as a class, we must not stop at England or Australia or America, or Germany, but think too of India, of China, of Burma, of Malaya. If we do that I don't think we'll feel so sure that Marx was wrong.

STREETER: I admit there are aspects of what Allen says that I haven't thought about. I'd like to go into them more fully, but I feel I ought to give South a chance.

CHAIRMAN: Yes, I think so. Now South.

SOUTH: I have already several times, in previous discussions, stated that I agree with Marx's determinism; so I'm not going to go over that. I'll concentrate on differences, and the first point I'd like to take up is this one of the 'dehumanization' of the proletariat, its being deprived of human privileges. I think it is a purely rhetorical expression. I don't think it has any exact meaning. It is a vague term that suits the purposes of Marx's argument. He wants to show that the proletariat will

have to bring about every necessary condition for full humanity. They will only do this if they themselves lack every vestige
of humanity, so that they won't be fully human unless they
themselves, in their revolution, create every single necessary
condition. It seems to me to be literally nonsense. It has no
meaning.

STREETER: All the same the conditions of the workers were
very bad in Marx's day.

SOUTH: I'm not denying that. Nevertheless, they were not
entirely deprived of rights. Their position was different from
that of slaves or serfs, for example. To say that they were
deprived of every human privilege (assuming that this means
something definite) is simply not true. And then there is the
further point that if, as Allen says, they gradually win rights
and privileges as a result of their struggle against capital, if they
gradually better their lot then, no matter how they started, at a
later stage in their struggle they no longer have the compul-
sion upon them to carry the revolution through, as Marx
argues. They come to have (even if they have not at the
beginning), vested interests to defend. So Marx's argument
does not stand up even if it were sound on other grounds
which it is not.

STREETER: How else do you think it falls down?

SOUTH: It falls down in his basic assumption that complete
deprivation of privileges leads people to revolt. The only ones
who revolt, and certainly the only ones who can carry through
successful revolutions and run society, are those who already
have enterprise. You don't develop enterprise if you have no
opportunities to exercise it. It is from those opportunities you
have, that you develop the capacity and the desire for more
exercise of enterprise, the capacity and the desire to go after it.

STREETER: Do you mean that that is why the bourgeoisie
were able to revolt but the workers will not be able to revolt?

SOUTH: The bourgeoisie would be one example on the
positive side. If, for the sake of argument, we accept the
Marxist view that there was a bourgeois revolution, then we
can say that the bourgeoisie were able to lead it because they
were already exercising enterprise in the running of their
businesses, their guilds, their towns, their churches. If they had
not been deprived of something they would not have revolted;

if they had not had something already they would not have been able to revolt.

STREETER: I see that. So you say the workers will not be able to make a successful revolution.

SOUTH: I have said nothing of the kind. What I have said is this: If Marx is right in saying the workers are completely dehumanized then this means that they cannot even get started on revolt. It is because they have certain social advantages—a decisive place in the economic structure, organization—such things as Marx himself points to, that they are able to struggle against oppressions.

STREETER: So you are saying that the workers *will* be able to make a successful revolution.

SOUTH: No. I am not saying that either. You want it all black or all white. It is a matter of history that the workers have organized, have conducted political and economic struggles, that they have succeeded in realizing some of their demands. We cannot deny that. But all that is still a long way from saying that they will be able to bring about a classless society or a society without oppressions.

STREETER: How would you judge whether they would do so or not?

SOUTH: I have no cut and dried prescription. In fact I don't think there is one. You have to examine the forces at work in contemporary society and see whither they are tending. You have to examine the workers themselves, how they run their own organizations, how they approach their problems, the consistency with which they oppose oppression as such and so on. I agree with Marx that in the course of the struggle some workers have developed their enterprise to a remarkable degree. Nevertheless, if we examine the working class as a whole and its political activity, and if we compare what we find with the qualities that would be required to establish a classless society, then I think we are forced to say that the workers are not displaying and give no sign of displaying anything remotely approaching the necessary qualities. In fact I think it is true to say that, as their material conditions improve, the workers lose interest in collectively shaping their own lives and in running society. You can see a deterioration in the workers' movement over the last fifty years.

ALLEN: That is a sweeping statement. It surely needs some support.

CHAIRMAN: Maybe, but I must ask South not to support it. We must consider our time. Carry on, South.

SOUTH: I agree with Allen that, if the workers are to emancipate themselves and the rest of society, then they can do it only if they themselves are organized democratically, are enlightened, make their own decisions collectively, and are not simply led or compelled by discipline from above. I agree with Allen that that is how the facts stand. I also agree with Allen that that is Marx's position. I disagree with Allen in this respect: I stress the '*if*'. Allen thinks this emancipation is bound to happen. In that belief he is a genuine Marxist. It is precisely there that I think he and Marx are wrong. I have already said why I think so.

STREETER: So you think Lenin was wrong?

SOUTH: Yes. I don't think there is any doubt about that. Lenin was certainly opposing Marxism in his theories of discipline although he spoke in the name of Marxism. And he was wrong on the facts of the case too. You cannot through rigid discipline lead men to freedom. The more the Communist Party made policy, the less fit the workers would be to run their own affairs. I agree with Allen, that the history of the Soviet Union confirms this view. There is far less freedom now than there was under the Czars. I know there is difference of opinion about that. Nevertheless for my part, I don't think there is any doubt about the facts.

STREETER: And what about the difficulty I was raising concerning the worsening of the conditions of the workers?

SOUTH: There is that question, and there is the question of the alleged division of society into two great camps—capitalist and worker. On this second question you will have no difficulty in foreseeing my views. I have put forward a pluralist theory of society. I have denied that political forces line up on one basis and one alone. Even where you have two main political parties in a society—one labour and the other anti-labour—all sorts of political tendencies play through each party. I have argued all that before, so I repudiate the 'two great camps' theory. Where a party claims that this is the position its claim is a weapon for establishing its own despotism. It is trying to make one issue supreme and all other issues subordinate to it—in other words, it is committed to a theory which, if logically followed out, involves the suppression of those forces for which the allegedly subordinate issues are, in fact, not subordinate at all but of the first importance. That is my view on the issue of the two great camps.

STREETER: I see that. Now what about the worsening of conditions?

SOUTH: On that, aren't both you and Allen right? There is no such thing as the conditions of the workers as a whole. There is the condition of these workers here and of those workers there. Some are up and some are down. Moreover, I don't think it is so simple that it can be attributed to the working out of Capitalism. All sorts of factors play their part. In Asia, for instance, we find worsening of conditions in places due to pressure of rapidly rising population with only primitive methods of production to cope with provision for this population. In various parts of the world rapid industrialization means that resources are going into capital goods —machines, factories, railways and so on—rather than into consumer goods. This happens whether the economy is capitalist or not. It happened in Britain during the industrial revolution, it has happened in Russia since the 1917 revolution. This is one reason why, in terms of consumer goods for the populace, Russia has not got back to the standard of living under the Czars.

CHAIRMAN: Once again a controversial assertion.

SOUTH: No doubt, but I believe the facts are so. However, my main point is that it is simply unscientific to pin such falls in standard of living on an economic system—capitalism, socialism or any other. They have a variety of causes. Political policy is another one I might mention. And further the position varies from place to place and from time to time. There is no such general worsening as Marx expected.

IX

The Dictatorship of the Proletariat

CHAIRMAN: We agreed at our last meeting that we would discuss the Marxist view of the workers and their position after the revolution—in other words the Marxist view of the Dictatorship of the Proletariat.

STREETER: It should not take us long to dispose of that, Mr. Chairman. I've been doing some reading about it and the whole theory seems to me to be obviously unsound.

ALLEN: Maybe this is just a case of a little knowledge being a dangerous thing. I'd very much like to hear what you think the theory is, and why you think it can be dismissed so lightly.

STREETER: I have never pretended to be an expert. All the same the theory of the dictatorship of the proletariat, as I understand it, fits in very well with the Marxist point of view as we've had it from Allen in our earlier discussions.

ALLEN: Naturally the Marxist theory of the Dictatorship of the Proletariat fits in with the rest of Marxist theory. Nevertheless, there are many misconceptions about it and I'll reserve my judgement on whether you have it right until I hear what you have to say.

CHAIRMAN: You are content then, Allen, that Streeter should give us his views on this topic before you give us your own?

ALLEN: Yes, Mr. Chairman. I think that procedure might be useful. If Streeter's interpretation is correct it will save me trouble and we can go on to consider the merits of the theory. If, on the other hand, he has accepted one of the misinterpretations of the theory, then it might serve to bring out some aspects of the real theory all the more clearly by way of corrections and contrast.

CHAIRMAN: Very well then. You have the floor, Streeter.

Go right ahead and state the position as you see it. Be as concise as possible.

STREETER: We have been told, in earlier discussions, that society is divided into conflicting classes. The state is the instrument of the ruling class and acts to keep the exploited classes in check, to maintain the economic dominance of the ruling class, that is to maintain the forms of property upon which its dominance is based. In our society we have capitalism as the economic system, capitalist forms of property, a capitalist ruling class and consequently a state which is the instrument of the dictatorship of the capitalist class. That is the Marxist theory as I have understood it so far.

Now let me go on from there. The capitalist system maintains the proletariat in being and also stimulates it to revolt. Eventually the proletarian revolution is successful. The capitalist state is overthrown and the dictatorship of the proletariat replaces it. The dictatorship of the proletariat does away with capitalist forms of property and substitutes socialist forms of property, that is public ownership of the means of production, distribution, and exchange. Unlike capitalist forms of property these socialist forms of property constitute no basis for the exploitation of man by man. Consequently, as capitalist ways of thinking die out, the dictatorship of the proletariat can be relaxed gradually, the workers' state itself gradually withers away—there being no need for a state where there are no classes to be kept in subjection—and eventually there is a stateless society, a truly human society, a classless society instead of a class society.

The period of the dictatorship of the proletariat is, however, a period when there is a need for a strong state, for in that period there are still hostile classes. The capitalists, though defeated, are nevertheless not yet destroyed. They continue to wield considerable economic power in the society. Consequently it is the task of the dictatorship firstly to break their economic power by switching over the economy as quickly as is practicable to a socialist economy and, secondly, to deprive them of the possibility of a capitalist restoration by breaking their political power, by disfranchizing them. However, the power of capitalism does not reside only in capitalists but it resides also in the fact that capitalist ideology has a strong grip on the minds of many workers who, contrary to their class interests, which they do not understand, will take or support political action which is in the interests of capitalism. The danger of a capitalist restoration is, therefore, not threatened simply from capitalists or former capitalists but arises also from parties which may be overwhelmingly working-class in membership and even leadership, but which, nevertheless, are deluded by capitalist ideology and which have policies that threaten the very existence of the socialist economy. The dictatorship of the proletariat must protect the real interests of the workers against these parties also by whatever means may be necessary.

Who then can exercise this dictatorship? Clearly only a party which understands the real interests of the workers and how they work out in history, only a party which understands Marxism, only the Communist Party. As trustees for the workers the Communist Party, using its superior insight into history gained from its identification of its own interests with those of the workers and from its knowledge of Marxism . . . wields the dictatorship of the proletariat. It has, of course, the general support of the proletariat but it may find that it is necessary to suppress this or that backward layer of workers, or this or that party whose membership is over-whelmingly proletarian but whose ideology and policy are bourgeois. Just as in a capitalist dictatorship we can find some capitalists suppressed politically, so in a proletarian dictatorship we can find some workers suppressed politically. The vital point is that the dictatorship is in the workers' interests. As time goes on the dictatorship can afford to relax its grip, capitalist ideology having declined in strength and capitalist economic forms having been destroyed. Then sets in the withering away of this last state. That is the theory of the dictatorship of the proletariat as I understand it.

ALLEN: But. . . .

CHAIRMAN: One moment, Allen, let Streeter finish.

STREETER: I say this theory is clearly unsound. I leave out the sort of criticisms that South will bring against it—denying that the moving political forces are classes and all that. I am prepared, for the sake of argument, to waive all those points. My criticism is that, if this state of affairs comes about, as it did come about in Russia, it is misleading to call it a dictatorship of the proletariat. It is a dictatorship of a party, it is a dictatorship over the proletariat as well as over other sections of the population. It doesn't matter if it is argued that the actions of the party are in the real interests of the workers. The party alone is allowed to determine what are the real interests of the workers. It tells the workers what are their real interests, and, if they happen to think differently, well that is just too bad for them. Even if the party was always right about this it would still be a dictatorship of the party and not of the workers. But, of course, we are making a very big assumption when we assume that the party will even attempt to go on ruling in the interest of the workers. Confronted with all the temptations of power, confronted with the opportunity to satisfy its own interests if necessary at the expense of the interests of the workers, are we to assume that the party has found such a formula for incorruptibility that it will never succumb to these temptations, that it will never serve its own interests at the expense of the interests of the workers? We shall find not merely that there is not a dictatorship of the proletariat but even that there is not a dictatorship of the party in the interests of the proletariat; rather there is a dictatorship of the party *against* the interests of the proletariat. The workers exploited under capitalism are now exploited by the Party.

Even that presents too favourable a picture. I have been speaking as if you could, under the given circumstances, have a dictatorship of the party. In fact you cannot. For the party to wield the dictatorship—the party as a whole—there would have to be democratic discussion and decision within the party. But you can't have that when the party is suppressing all dissenting views and policies outside itself. For one thing the habits of mind required in the two cases are quite different. For another thing you could not preserve the unity of the party under these circumstances. If any policy gains widespread adherence outside the party, especially in the social groups the party is supposed to represent, it is certain that it will gain some adherents within the party. Those who accept it within the party will not want to see it suppressed outside. Their own pressing of it within the party must strengthen it outside and help to threaten the dominant policy within the party. The party leadership, upholding the dominant policy as in the interests of the workers, must regard this alternative policy as mistaken and, therefore, objectively speaking (if not in intention), as being opposed to the interests of the workers, and, therefore, as one to be suppressed. (The dictatorship of the proletariat on this whole approach must mean the dictatorship of one policy over alternative policies). Consequently the party leadership must oppose all factions and groupings within the party because they could only be factions and groupings against the party's policy—that is, against the interests of the workers. And that banning of factions within the party is what has happened in Russia. If you try to establish a dictatorship of the party in the interests of the proletariat you end up with a dictatorship of the leadership within and over the party and over the proletariat as well. All that seems to me perfectly clear. It is what you would expect, and it is what has happened in Russia. That is why I say that the Marxist theory of the Dictatorship of the Proletariat is unsound. As a description of what will happen it is obviously unsound. Instead of the weakening of the dictatorship you find it grows stronger; instead of the withering away of the State you find it grows greater. And at no stage is it a workers' dictatorship or a workers' state.

CHAIRMAN: Thank you, Streeter. Now, Allen, have you anything to say to that?

ALLEN: Yes, I have. I am glad Streeter said all that, although I must confess I was impatient of it in parts because he was barking up the wrong tree. That is not criticism of Marxism. Marx's theory of the Dictatorship of the Proletariat is nothing like that. Marx himself would have made all Streeter's criticisms of the theory Streeter called Marxist.

STREETER: How is that? You'll find all that I said in the writings of Lenin and Trotsky.

ALLEN: Yes, you'll find it all in the writings of Lenin and Trotsky. You'll find it in Stalin too. But you won't find it in Marx or Engels, and, after all, it's Marxism we're talking about. These people called themselves Marxists, but we don't have to take them at their own words. Fortunately, we have Marx's and Engels' own texts and we can see for ourselves the Marxist doctrine of the dictatorship of the proletariat.

STREETER: Well I'm always willing to learn. What is the Marxist doctrine?

ALLEN: I think it can be conclusively demonstrated that it differs fundamentally from the Bolshevik doctrine which retains the Marxist phrase 'dictatorship of the proletariat' but not the Marxist meaning. You ought to realize, from the discussions we have already had, that Marx and Engels use the word 'dictatorship' in a special sense. For example they describe a capitalist regime as a capitalist dictatorship, even if politically it is a democracy, even if there is universal suffrage, freedom of speech, freedom of organization and so on. Thus they would describe Australia or Britain or the United States of America as capitalist dictatorships, but they would not mean by this that one party alone—and that a capitalist party—could exist, that members of non-capitalist classes were deprived of political rights or anything of that kind. When they spoke of a capitalist dictatorship they meant simply that the state defended capitalist property rights, but this is quite compatible with a democratic political form.

STREETER: It seems to me to be a peculiar way to use the word 'dictatorship'.

ALLEN: I admit that. Not only is it peculiar but I think it is most unfortunate. It has left the way open for the kind of misinterpretations that have been put upon it by such people as - the Bolsheviks. In my opinion the word 'hegemony' would have been much better and not so easily misinterpreted. However, in the writings of Marx and Engels—apart from the word 'dictatorship'—there is no justification whatever for the Bolshevik interpretation which you stated for us. In fact there is the clear statement of an opposing interpretation.

STREETER: You mean that just as a political democracy with a capitalist class dominant in it was called a capitalist dictatorship, so Marx and Engels, when they spoke of the dictatorship of the proletariat, meant a political democracy with the working class dominant.

ALLEN: Yes, that is exactly what I do mean.

STREETER: I can see from what you have said, that such an interpretation is possible but I'm certain that you have not demonstrated that it is the correct one.

ALLEN: I admit that, but I can do so and I will go on with

that job now. Let us go right back to the *Manifesto of the Communist Party* which Marx and Engels wrote in 1848. There they say: 'The first stage in the working class revolution is the constitution of the proletariat as the ruling class, the conquest of democracy.'

That seems to me to be quite unambiguous. Marx and Engels believed that the workers constituted the overwhelming majority of the population. Once this overwhelming majority had become class-conscious, democracy would ensure that it was the ruling class. It would have no need of suppression of the political rights of other sections of the population. Given its own class-consciousness, its numbers would ensure its dominance so long as it maintained democracy.

Moreover, the working class would need to maintain democracy in its own ranks if it was to rule. The proletariat is a multitude. Its will cannot be determined except by discussion and organizing and voting among its members. So, if the proletariat is to be the ruling class, it needs democracy in its own ranks and it does not need to abolish democratic rights for others. Those are the plain facts of the case and they support what Marx and Engels said in plain language in the quotation I have just given you.

STREETER: I can follow all that well enough, but isn't it significant that, in that quotation, Marx and Engels don't use the expression 'the dictatorship of the proletariat'.

ALLEN: No, it is not significant at all. They are talking about a certain stage in history, namely 'the first stage in the working class revolution'. 'The dictatorship of the proletariat' is a name they occasionally use to designate that first stage. But what they say about it applies whatever name they give to it. Indeed, the phrase 'dictatorship of the proletariat' is of little importance in the writings of Marx and Engels or, in fact, in the writings of their followers down to 1917. It was the Bolsheviks who gave it a new meaning and great importance, but they did so only by departing from the Marxist meaning.

STREETER: You may be right, but your case would be more convincing if you gave us examples of the use of the phrase by Marx and Engels themselves.

ALLEN: I will give you not only examples; I will give you

every single instance of their use of that phrase. Between them, in all their writings, they used it only five times. Marx used it three times, Engels used it twice. I'm afraid that the three instances from Marx don't help us one way or the other. He uses the phrase without expansion or explanation. However, if we remember that it is simply the name for the first stage of the proletarian revolution we can see clearly that for him it means democracy. When we come to Engels this is placed beyond all possible doubt. Engels is clear and unequivocal. The dictatorship of the proletariat means democracy. Firstly, then, let me state Marx's own passages. Though they don't support my interpretation they certainly don't oppose it and they bring no support for the Bolshevik interpretation you have put up.

1. In his book *Class Struggles in France*, 1850, Marx wrote:

. . . . the proletariat rallies more and more round revolutionary socialism, round communism, for which the bourgeoisie has itself found the name of Blanqui. This socialism is the declaration of the permanence of the revolution, the class dictatorship of the revolution, the class dictatorship of the proletariat as the inevitable transit point to the abolition of class differences generally. . . .

2. In a letter to Weydemeyer in 1852 Marx wrote:

What I did that was new was to prove: 1. that the existence of classes is only bound up with the particular historic phases in the development of production; 2. that the class struggle necessarily leads to the dictatorship of the proletariat; 3. that this dictatorship itself only constitutes the transition to the abolition of all classes and to a classless society.

3. Then we find in Marx's *Critique of the Gotha Programme* (1875):

Between capitalist and communist society lies the period of the revolutionary transformation of the one into the other. There corresponds to this also a political transition period in which the state can be nothing but *the revolutionary dictatorship of the proletariat*.

Those are Marx's three uses of the phrase.

STREETER: I agree with you that they tell us practically nothing about its meaning. You say Engels is more explicit?

ALLEN: Yes, he is quite explicit on the two occasions he uses it.

1. In 1891 he wrote a preface to Marx's *Civil War in France* and he wound up with these words: 'The German Philistine invariably falls into a holy terror at the words, dictatorship of the proletariat. Do you want to know, gentlemen, what that dictatorship really means? Take a look at the Commune of Paris. That is the dictatorship of the proletariat'.

STREETER: How does that help us?

ALLEN: Obviously. Accept Engels' advice. 'Take a look at the Commune of Paris'. There we find a democratic regime elected by universal suffrage. Not only did it contain working-class parties other than the Marxists—these other parties even overwhelmingly outnumbered the Marxists. Nor was this all. There were representatives of parties which were not working-class at all but opposed to it—class enemies. In other words the Commune was a democratic republic—one in which working-class parties (I stress the plural) were in a majority. It is this which Engels points to as the dictatorship of the proletariat.

2. Two months later he put the matter beyond all doubt in his criticism of the draft programme of German social democracy:

If anything is certain it is that our party and the working class can only come to power under the form of a democratic republic. Precisely this is the specific form for the dictatorship of the proletariat, as the Great French Revolution has already shown.

That needs no explanation. It is decisive in itself.

STREETER: What you say seems to be sound, but, if it is so, I cannot understand why Marx and Engels used the term 'dictatorship'. Surely it lends itself to misconstruction.

ALLEN: I have already said that I consider it an unfortunate term. All the same you can't expect Marx and Engels to foresee and provide against every misinterpretation to which their works would be subjected. However, even if they had foreseen the misconstructions that would follow, while they would, no doubt, have gone to much greater pains to explain and amplify, they might, nevertheless, have stuck to the word 'dictatorship'. After all, it was no accident that they used it.

STREETER: If it was no accident it certainly needs some explanation. It seems queer to me that when they mean 'democracy' they say 'dictatorship'.

ALLEN: It may seem queer, but, as I've demonstrated, that is exactly what they do. And when we look into the position it is not as queer as it seems at first sight. On the one hand, the rule of the workers can be exercised only in a democracy. But on the other hand they want to stress that any state—any state at all—relies on the use of force to defend certain property rights. The capitalist state (even if it is a democracy) uses force to protect capitalist property rights. Similarly the workers' state will use force to protect socialist property rights and, where necessary, to expropriate the capitalists. That is the element of force in any state whether it is democratic or not. And Marx and Engels want to keep the point clear that this is always present so long as there is a class society. The dictatorship of the proletariat—though it is democratic—will not have the voluntary compliance of all members of society, especially on property questions. It will find it necessary to enforce the will of the majority on a minority who otherwise would refuse to comply with the will of the majority. But that does not mean that the minority has to be deprived of political rights. After all, in our society I am quite free to advocate that I should be given the right to buy the Sydney Harbour Bridge for a pound and thereafter have exclusive rights to charge tolls for the use of it. I am free to advocate that. I can stand for Parliament on that platform. I can try to organize a party in support of it. Politically, I can exercise my democratic rights in the matter. But if I try to expropriate the Sydney Harbour Bridge, if I set up a toll barrier and order off the painters and try in fact to exercise any of the rights of private ownership, then the State will use its police force to restrain me. On the one hand we have the democratic aspect of our society; on the other its 'dictatorship'. Marx and Engels are saying: Don't forget that in any state force is always present, and it will be present in the state of the workers too, despite the fact that that state will be more democratic than any hitherto existing. That is why they use the word 'dictatorship'.

STREETER: I see that, but I still think it is very misleading. However, I won't dwell on it. There is just one other question I'd like to ask. I noticed that in your third quotation from Marx he said 'the revolutionary dictatorship of the proletariat'. What is the special force of that word 'revolutionary'?

ALLEN: I thought that would have been clear from our previous discussions. The workers' state, once it has been achieved, will busy itself with changing property relations, with the expropriation of capitalist ownership of the means of production and the establishing of social ownership. This will be a gradual process. It is also a truly revolutionary process because it changes the economic foundations of society and will result in the transformation of the superstructure of society. It is a revolution which is permanent, in the sense that it will not cease until a fully classless society has been established and the state has completely withered away. Then truly human history as opposed to class history will begin.

CHAIRMAN: Thank you, Allen. Perhaps that would be an appropriate point for you to finish and for South to begin any criticisms he may wish to make.

SOUTH: I agree that Streeter correctly stated the Bolshevik theory of the dictatorship of the proletariat. I also agree with his criticisms of it. But I also agree with Allen that it is not the Marxist theory and that the Marxist theory is as he says. I think his quotations settle that point. However, I think the Marxist theory is itself unsound and that, maybe not merely through the misleading effects of the word 'dictatorship', it can be twisted into the Bolshevik theory.

ALLEN: But you've just admitted that it is different from the Bolshevik theory.

SOUTH: Oh, yes. Don't misunderstand me. They are different theories. The Bolshevik theory of the dictatorship of the proletariat is different in important respects from the Marxist theory. What I am saying is that there are weaknesses in the Marxist theory which lend themselves to the development of the Bolshevik theory and that these weaknesses go much deeper than the unfortunate choice of the word—'dictatorship'.

ALLEN: Then it's up to you to show the weaknesses.

SOUTH: Quite. That is what I'll try to do. As Streeter

predicted, I cannot accept the class theory of the state. No state can be described simply as the instrument of a class. I've given my reasons for saying that before, and I won't repeat them now.

Secondly, no class is a politically homogeneous force. There is no such thing as the policy of the proletariat. The proletariat doesn't have a policy and shows no signs of developing one. It has many policies, i.e. its different sections have different policies, some of which are irreconcilable.

Thirdly, even if the majority of the proletariat favoured a policy of nationalization of the means of production and if this was carried through, it would result in a centralization of economic power which would increase the power of the state rather than lead to its withering away. Any alternative form of social ownership of the means of production has negligible support among the workers. So the notion of a dictatorship of the proletariat which will lead to a withering away of the state and to a classless society free from exploitation finds no support in the facts of existing society.

Fourthly, there is nothing to show that the workers as a class have developed or are developing interest in or knowledge of general social problems so that they have general social policies. They may have policies on wages and hours and a few other matters of that kind. But they have, for example, no general economic policy, no general foreign policy, no policy with regard to culture, no policy on constitutional or legal questions and no interest in developing such policies. No doubt from their ranks support will come for this or that group which has such policies but largely for irrelevant reasons—because such policies are linked with wages or taxation policies of which they approve or something of that kind—not because they have looked into the problems themselves. This simply means that the proletariat will not be a ruling class. It remains (except in a few respects) a led class and a gullible class. As its political power has increased (in the sense of the numerical weight of its votes and its economic strength through strike action), it has used that power not to establish its own rule (which would involve tremendously heightened political consciousness and activity), but to transfer power from private capital to hierarchies of officials of one kind and another.

I agree with Marx to this extent: if there were to be a dictatorship of the proletariat it could come about only by an intense political consciousness and activity within a democratic framework on the part of the proletariat. But my criticism is that this is not happening. His account of the future is Utopian.

STREETER: Even if all that you say is true, you have not shown that the weaknesses in the Marxist theory give rise to the Bolshevik type of theory.

SOUTH: I see that in this way: it is not a matter of the Marxist theory logically giving rise to the Bolshevik theory. The Bolshevik theory is indefensible from the Marxist point of view. But politically the pressure from one to the other is very great. Suppose that the criticism I have made above is sound, that a Marxist party gets into power pledged to a Marxist policy. Naturally they will expect continued support and even pressure from the workers in the direction of socialism, in the direction of workers' government and so on. As a Marxist party they must believe that that will happen. If my criticisms are sound it won't happen. What is the party to do? It can either say openly: the theory on which our policy is based is wrong, we'll have to think again; or it can say: our theory is right; this is the dictatorship of the proletariat; the rule of our party is the dictatorship of the proletariat because it is in the interests of the workers though unfortunately many workers are still so backward that they go against their own interests and so will have to be forced.

I think it is worth considering what Max Eastman has to say on this question in *Stalin's Russia and the Crisis in Socialism*. Eastman quotes from Rosa Luxemburg's criticism of the Bolsheviks:

The basic error of the Lenin-Trotskyist theory is simply this: that they set dictatorship, just as Kautsky does, over against democracy. 'Dictatorship or democracy'—that is the question both for the Bolsheviks and for Kautsky. Kautsky decides, naturally, for democracy. . . . Lenin and Trotsky decide for dictatorship in opposition to democracy and, in so doing, for the dictatorship of a handful of individuals, that is, for dictatorship after the bourgeois fashion. Two opposite poles, both equally removed from the true socialist policy.

When the proletariat seizes power, it cannot follow Kautsky's advice and renounce the job of carrying through a socialist transformation, under pretext of the unripeness of the country, and devote itself merely to democracy, without committing treason to itself, to the International and to the Revolution. It is bound to and must without delay, in the most vigorous, unwavering and thorough-going manner, take socialist measures in hand, hence exercise dictatorship—but dictatorship of the class, not of a party or clique; dictatorship of the class, that is, in the broadest publicity, with the active participation of the masses, in unlimited democracy.

And Eastman comments:

. . . . My assertion that Luxemburg, if confronted by the same crisis, would have done the same thing (as Lenin and Trotsky) . . . is not a psychoanalytic impertinence, but an inference from what she says:

The working class *'is bound to and must without delay, in the most vigorous, unwavering and thorough-going manner, take socialist measures'*, but it must take them as 'a class', not 'a party', and still less 'a clique' it must take them 'in the broadest publicity', 'with the active participation of the masses', 'in unlimited democracy'.

It is bound to and must—but suppose it doesn't! What are you going to do then? That is the real question and it was never answered by Rosa Luxemburg. It could not be answered by her, because she was a 'true believer' in the Marxian religion, and for a true believer such a question cannot arise. The proletariat . . . 'is bound to and must' . . . When the real proletariat . . . fails to act 'without delay, in the most vigorous, unwavering and thoroughgoing manner', as it usually will fail, is there much doubt what a mystic believer in its historic destiny . . . will do?

What Eastman brings out in this passage is that the falseness of the Marxist predictions about the proletariat put the Marxist party in this dilemma: either they must confess the Marxist theory has turned out to be wrong or they must twist the Marxist theory into its Bolshevik interpretation. The first course simply wrecks the party—a few individuals may take it, but hardly the party as a whole eager to fulfil Marxist prophecies. The second course produces all the consequences mentioned by Streeter. It is, of course, possible to say: the proletariat is not ready yet. In that case the Marxist party soon has its Marxism corrupted and becomes simply another Labour Party. In practical politics the theory of the dictatorship of the proletariat leads Marxist parties into a political dead-end as far as Marxist political aims are concerned.

X

The Work of the Marxist Party

CHAIRMAN: This is the last of our discussions. I believe we agreed to discuss the Marxist conception of the function of the Marxist or Communist Party.

ALLEN: That is so, Mr. Chairman, but I think it might be more accurate to refer simply to the Marxist Party. Not all Marxist parties have been called Communist. For example, most Marxist parties for a long time called themselves Social Democratic parties. On the other hand, not all Communist Parties have been Marxist, not even all those Communist parties which have claimed to be Marxist.

CHAIRMAN: The main point is that we understand what we mean. I take it that we are all agreed that we are concerned with a party which is based on Marxist theories and which is following Marxist policies.

SOUTH: We are concerned with Marx's view of how such a party would work, what it would do and how it would do it.

ALLEN: Exactly.

CHAIRMAN: Then we are agreed, and if anyone says simple 'the Party,' we shall know what he has in mind.

STREETER: After the way Allen treated what I had to say last time, I feel some diffidence about putting forward what I have read, especially as, once again, what I have to put forward are the ideas of Lenin. Is Allen going to say that his ideas on the Party, like his ideas on the Dictatorship of the Proletariat, are not Marxist?

ALLEN: I most certainly do say exactly that. Lenin is as much a heretic on the question of the Party as he is on the question of the Dictatorship of the Proletariat, and his anti-Marxism in each case springs from the same source.

SOUTH: I agree with Allen on that point. All the same, I

think the Leninist position ought to be stated. It is the position which most people who have not made a special study of the question think is the Marxist position and, further, I believe it does bring out the real Marxist position more clearly by contrast.

ALLEN: Quite so.

CHAIRMAN: Very well, if you both think so, we shall hear the results of Streeter's reading.

STREETER: Whether they are Marxist or not, Lenin's ideas seemed to me to be striking and consistent. In *What is to be Done?* he says:

The working class exclusively, by its own efforts, is able to develop only trade-union consciousness . . . Modern socialist consciousness can only be brought to them from without . . ., can arise only on the basis of profound scientific knowledge. The bearers of science are not the proletariat but the bourgeois intelligentsia. It is out of the heads of members of this stratum that modern socialism originated . . . Pure and simple trade unionism means the ideological subordination of the workers to the bourgeoisie . . . Our task is to bring the labor movement under the wing of revolutionary Social Democracy . . . Working-class consciousness cannot be genuinely political consciousness unless the workers are trained to respond to all classes of tyranny, oppression, violence and abuse, no matter what *class* is affected . . . To bring political knowledge to the workers, the Social Democrats must *go among all classes of the population*, must dispatch units of their army *in all directions*. The Social Democrats' ideal should not be a trade-union secretary, but *a tribune of the people*.

One interesting aspect of Lenin's views is his stress on the intellectuals. It is true he does not exclude workers from his organization. On the contrary, he welcomes them. But he thought they would be only 'exceptional workingmen'. They would find it harder to develop 'full social-democratic consciousness' but they would have the advantage of knowing intimately the psychology of the workers. 'The organizations of revolutionists must be comprised first and foremost of people whose profession is that of revolutionist . . . As this is the common feature of the members of such an organization, *all distinctions as between workers and intellectuals* must be dropped.'

He laid great stress on the professional side. He wrote,

I assert, 1. That no movement can be durable without a stable organisation of leaders to maintain continuity; 2. That the more widely the masses are drawn into the struggle and form the basis of the movement, the more it is necessary to have such an organisation and the more stable it must be; 3. that the organisation must consist chiefly of persons engaged in revolution as a profession. . . .

In *What is to be Done?* Lenin stresses the need not only for knowledge, but also for centralized discipline in the party.

In *The Infantile Disease of Leftism* he included a passage which seems to me to illuminate his conception of the nature and function of the party. It refers to the period after the party is in power, but fits in with his conception of the function of the party during the period before it comes to power, the function he allotted to the party in *What is to be Done?*. Lenin wrote:

The dictatorship of the proletariat is a relentless struggle . . . against the forces and traditions of the old society. The force of habit of millions and tens of millions is a most formidable force. Without a party of iron, tempered in struggle, without a party possessing the confidence of all that is honest in the class in question, without a party able to detect the moods of the mass and influence it, it is impossible to wage such a struggle with success . . .

Not one important political or organisational question is decided by any state institution in our republic without the governing instruction of the central committee of the party.

Now, from the quotations I have given and from many others in the works I have been reading, this is how I think Lenin conceived the Party:

It is a centralized, tightly-disciplined organization, most of whose leading members are professional revolutionists. Its members understand the historical process as expounded by Marx, and they have to bring this understanding to the workers who would never arrive at it by themselves. Even with the work of the party, it seems that many of the workers don't arrive at that understanding, even after the party has attained power. The party has to study their moods and influence them. Also, of course, after it is in power, it gives orders to State institutions. Major decisions are taken, not in those institutions, but in the central committee of the party. Another interesting aspect is Lenin's view that the party should go among all classes of the population and have as its ideal a tribune of the people.

Now, both Allen and South say quite confidently that this is not Marxist. They may be right, but I'd certainly like to hear them answer this point: that it is Marxism applied to Russia. Lenin had to deal with the special Russian situation and it certainly could not be done simply by applying a formula.

CHAIRMAN: Well, Streeter, I've just been reading Max Eastman's book, *Marxism, is it Science?*. In that book, Eastman gives substantially the same account of the Leninist function of the party as you give, but he insists that it is not Marxist. I know Allen is going to tell us that Marx was right and Lenin wrong. It is interesting that Eastman expresses the view that Lenin was right and Marx wrong, although he warns us in a note that he later became much more critical of Lenin. He deals with the problem in Chapters entitled 'The Bolshevik Heresy' and 'Lenin as an Engineer of Revolution'. It is that expression, 'Engineer of Revolution', which is the key to his view. Lenin saw the revolution as something which had to be brought about or engineered, and the party was the great instrument for engineering it:

Lenin founded his Bolshevik organisation upon a recognition of the *indispensable* historic function of a group of people who were not defined according to the economic class to which they belonged, but were defined according to their purposive activity and their state of mind. They were people committed and consecrated to a certain social purpose—but with this difference . . . that they possessed the Marxian science and the Marxian technique for the achievement of that purpose. In short, they were revolutionary engineers. . . .

Lenin corrected the error of Marx which was a mystic faith in the proletariat as such . . . He denied both the (Marxist theories) assertion that the material elements of the world are automatically evolving towards socialism, and its assertion that the thoughts of socialists are a mere reflection of the process . . . The substance of Hegelian Marxism is the assertion that the proletariat *as such*, by virtue of a dialectic necessity inherent in its elemental and material nature, is bound to fight the bourgeoisie and achieve the revolution, and that ideas and theories in the minds of socialists can be nothing but a reflection of the process. . . .

The leading Russian Marxist, Plekhanov, in *The Working Class and The Social Democratic Intelligentsia*,

said that Lenin's popularity was due to a 'departure from Marxism which made his ideas accessible to those "practicals" who are unprepared to understand Marxism.' He proved this with a quotation from Marx: 'It is not a question of what goal this or that proletarian sets himself at a given time, or even the whole proletariat. It is a question of what the class is in itself, and of what, in view of this its being, it is historically bound to accomplish.'

He reminded his readers that, according to the philosophy of historical materialism, 'Economic necessity gives birth to and carries to its logical end—that is, to the social revolution—that movement of the working class of which scientific socialism serves as a theoretic expression'. And he excommunicated Lenin from the true church of this philosophy in these words:

The disputed question consists in this: Does there exist an economic necessity which calls forth in the proletariat a demand for socialism, makes it instinctively socialistic, and impels it—even if left to its own resources—on the road to social revolution, notwithstanding the stubborn and continual effort of the bourgeoisie to subject it to its own ideological influence? Lenin denies this, in face of the clearly expressed opinions of all the theorists of scientific socialism. And in that consists his enormous mistake, his theoretical fall into sin.

And a little later, Eastman says:

No matter what the passing situation may be, a dialectic materialist is bound to conceive the revolution as automatically produced by the contradictions in capitalism, and the Marxian leader as 'bringing consciousness' to the process, or 'serving as its theoretical expression'. At the most, he may permit this Marxian leader to accidentally accelerate the movement. There is not a word in Lenin's book which is even a concession to this metaphysical ideology. The book tells you 'what to do', if you want to produce with the material at hand a socialist revolution. It is a textbook of practical engineering on the basis of the Marxian analysis of history. Lenin was indeed 'organically incapable of dialectic thinking', in so far as dialectic thinking means attributing your own purposes to the external world.

I thought I'd quote these passages from Eastman because they do bring out sharply two different conceptions of the function of the party. In Lenin's conception it engineers the revolution. In Marx's, the revolution will happen anyway.

The party merely helps to bring the consciousness of what is happening to the workers and thereby may speed up events. But they would learn from events in any case, and even need the assistance of events to understand what the party says.

I should add, before I finish, that Eastman, when he changed his view about Lenin, criticized him not because he (Eastman) came to think Marx was right, but because he came to think that Lenin was more deeply tied up with Marxism than he had at first believed. Marxism itself, Eastman believes to be a religious view. As he says, in his first Chapter, 'The World as Escalator,'

> Marxists profess to reject religion in favour of science, but they cherish a belief that the external universe is evolving with reliable, if not divine necessity in exactly the direction in which they want it to go. They do not conceive themselves as struggling to build the communist society in a world which is of its own nature indifferent to them. They conceive themselves as travelling toward that society in a world which is like a moving stairway taking them the way they walk. Their enemies are walking the same stairway, but walking in the wrong direction. This is not a scientific, but, in the most technical sense, a religious conception of the world.

At the time he wrote his other Chapters from which I have quoted, Eastman thought that Lenin was freer from this 'religious conception' than he later believed. What Eastman withdraws is not his endorsement of the 'engineering' approach as the scientific one, but his endorsement of Lenin as an adequate representative of it.

ALLEN: That is just where I join issue with him, but first let me answer Streeter's suggestion that Lenin's conception of the party was Marxism applied to Russia. On that point I think Eastman is right. The two approaches are diametrically opposed. If it was necessary to engineer the situation as Lenin and his party tried to do, it meant Russia was not ripe for the Socialist revolution and this is what the genuine Marxists (including Plekhanov) said at the time.

Just how far the unripeness of Russia forced the Bolsheviks to deviate from Marxism is shown by a statement made by Trotsky in *Pravda* on February 2, 1926. This statement is quoted by Eastman in a footnote to the Chapters you, Mr. Chairman, have been citing:

The social form of our industry is immeasurably higher than that of the United States. There a mad capitalist exploitation and the most terrible 'inequality of classes; here a form of industry such as opens the road to full equality of living conditions for the whole people. But in America in the frame of the capitalist form, there exists the highest technique. With us in the frame of the socialist or transitional form, an extremely backward technique. And the extent of that backwardness we ought to keep constantly before our eyes: not in order to drop our hands in despair but in order to double our efforts in the struggle for technique and culture . . . The technique of America combined with the Soviet social regime would give us not only socialism—it would give us communism, or at least it would bring very close those conditions of life in which each would work according to his abilities and receive according to his needs.

And Eastman comments: 'A more perfect contradiction of the Marxian philosophy of history, according to which social forms are "determined" by the evolving technique of industry, could hardly be imagined' (which is quite correct—but then he adds:) '—nor a more sensible attitude to the actual problem.'

Trotsky's attitude as expressed in this quotation is exactly that of Lenin. They and their party are going to *make* history go along a certain path. By 'doubling their efforts' to influence the masses by purposive activity, by 'governing instructions' of the party, by 'a party of iron' made up of professional revolutionists, which brings socialism to workers who would never arrive at it themselves—in short, by the knowledge and will of a minority, of the tightly-disciplined party, they are going to bring about socialism. And Eastman thinks this is 'a more sensible attitude to the whole problem' than is the attitude of Marx. And when the whole enterprise runs off the rails and produces results quite different from what they expect, Lenin can think of only a few minor organizational changes at the top, Trotsky talks about the *Revolution Betrayed*, and Eastman thinks Lenin didn't get far enough away from Marxism. I put it to you, Mr. Chairman, that it will be worthwhile considering whether his mistake didn't consist precisely in the fact that he did get away from Marxism, that he substituted the discipline, the knowledge, the will, and the rule of the party for the laws of history, that he tried to dictate to history instead of making history conscious of itself. After all, the genuine Marxists predicted where Lenin's party would finish up. They predicted it as soon as he stated his conception of the party. (Eastman has given the example of Plekhanov but there are plenty of others.)

The party is much more important for Lenin than for Marx. For Marx, the party's function is primarily educational—to point out what is happening, to be history conscious of itself and to be the agent whereby that consciousness becomes more widespread. For Marx, the party is not the moving force of history. The moving force of history is the economic structure of society—the material forces of production and the organization of men in production. Changes of ideas—in the working class or in any other class—are the result not of the work of the party but of changes in the economic structure.

I admit that Lenin and Trotsky and the other Bolsheviks learned a great deal from Marx. They learned something about the importance of economic structure and how it influences other factors. But, in this matter of the party, they missed the crucial point. They missed the whole force of Marx's rejection of Utopian socialism and his substitution of scientific socialism. What, in essence, is the Leninist approach if not a Utopian approach? The workers, left to themselves, will not develop socialist consciousness. The Party, a devoted group, which has seen the light, is going to tell them and bring about the socialist society. This is Utopianism pure and simple. It is true they dilute the Utopianism with a bit of Marxism but only to this extent: the party is going to grasp the levers of society and manipulate it, and it is Marx who has taught them which are the right levers. But what Marx taught was that they are not levers at all, they are not things that can be manipulated. They are natural forces. That is the meaning of 'scientific'.

Now, Max Eastman finds the Leninist approach a sensible one, more sensible than the Marxist approach. I am not surprised at this because he is an American and America—the United States—is the great country of technology. Eastman is applauding Lenin's technological approach to society—or, as he calls it, his engineering approach. But even in technology, the technologist can't do what he likes. He is limited by the nature of his materials and physical laws according to which they work. If the materials and their ways of working will fit into the pattern that he wants, then he can achieve his end. Otherwise he can't. In technological cases, the human agent can be a very important factor in the situation, but, even so, there are limits, very strict limits to what he can do—a fact which we tend to overlook because a competent technologist has in mind approximately what is practicable and what is not, and does not even try to do the impossible. How much more limited are the social possibilities of a party? It can't simply manipulate society. Society has its own laws of development and you must accept these. You can't do anything else. If you want to bring about any social result, you must work within those laws, co-operate with them, and that puts very strict limits to what you can do. And there is another very important point, too. Don't forget that the party itself is subject to social laws; it cannot stand above history and mould it. It is itself moulded. The other forces in society mould it, the very courses of action upon which it launches itself mould it.

Let me give you an example of what I mean. The Bolshevik Party—later known as the Communist Party—set out to bring about a society of the free and equal (a classless society) within a country not ripe for it. They were going to do it in a country not ripe for it—a backward country. They were going to do it by seizing and holding state power and directing things in the way they wanted them to go. But see what happens, see what is bound to happen. In order to hold power, the Party must maintain a dictatorship. In order to maintain a dictatorship, the Party must develop certain habits of mind—suppression of free criticism, defence of privilege (in the first instance, political privilege, but inevitably soon other forms of privilege), the habit of mind which relies on forcing results ('doubling our efforts'), not permitting them to grow spontaneously. Consequently, the time comes when the party is no longer interested in a society of the free and equal. It is no longer manipulating society for that purpose, but simply for the purpose of maintaining its own power. And if some individuals do keep in mind the original purpose and do protest against the deviations from it, their protests are futile because the social laws at work are building up within the party an attitude of mind which is hostile to their approach. That is what happened to

Trotsky. It is what would have happened to Lenin had he lived. They were sincere men who wanted the socialist society but the method they adopted defeated them. The very party which they believed could bring about their end, turned out to be the agent of forces opposed to that end. Trotsky was thrown out and murdered. Lenin's last despairing struggles against the degeneration of his party were futile. Their earlier comrades in arms—the old Bolsheviks—were almost entirely wiped out by the great purges of the 1930s. And Russia is further away from the classless society of which they dreamed than ever. It is pointless for Trotsky to talk about the 'Revolution Betrayed'. No doubt you can point out how Stalin and others personally betrayed their earlier ideas. But this betrayal is not the cause of degeneration. It is the effect of it. If Stalin hadn't been prepared to betray his ideas, he would have met the same fate as Trotsky, and someone else would have been held up as the arch-betrayer. The cause is in the kind of Party Lenin created and the kind of role he allotted to it. And, of course, this in itself had its causes—in the backwardness of Russian society. Those who set out to mould history are inevitably moulded by it, and the little bit of difference that they are able to make is in a reactionary direction. Those who set out to hurry history along, to make it jump over epochs, inevitably, if they have any effect, impede it. The great historical forces work themselves out and no party can change the laws of history.

There is no mystery about what happened to Lenin's plans. Max Eastman may be wise after the event (at least to the extent of seeing that Lenin was wrong, though he is no wiser in seeing *where* he was wrong), but the Marxists were wise before the event—from the very first publication of Lenin's ideas. They saw exactly where it would finish up. They saw this because they were scientific, because they recognized that a party cannot dictate to history but that it is at best an expression of history. If it is an expression of the progressive forces in history, of forces which it did not create but which created it, then it will let those forces roll along to their final goal, describing what is happening, being used by those forces, helping, as expression of those forces, to remove impediments to them, but no more. That is the function which Marxism allots to the party and it is in line with the scientific nature of the Marxist approach.

For Marx the decisive social force in the political sphere is not the party but the class, the proletariat which is forced by circumstances into revolt and into an increasing consciousness of its political tasks. This is in flat contradiction to Lenin's approach. The Communists, of course, differ from the rest of the proletariat in that they understand the whole historic process. (I mean here Marxist Communists, not present-day Stalinist Communists.) They say what they perceive and this helps the rest of the proletariat to catch on more quickly. But the rest of the proletariat is catching on because history is pushing it in that direction, because the Communists merely formulate what the proletariat is already groping for and what it is bound finally to learn. The function of the Communists for Marx is twofold—firstly to share the struggles of the workers because whatever mistakes the workers make, they are the progressive class, and secondly to teach, to point out to the workers the lessons of each of their struggles and to keep before their minds the fundamental problem. For Marx, the Communists are the agents not the moulders of history. Thus, in the *Manifesto of the Communist Party*, he writes:

The communists everywhere support every revolutionary movement against extant social and political conditions.

In all these movements, the communists bring the property question to the fore, regarding it as fundamental, no matter what phase of development it may happen to be in.

Communists scorn to hide their views and aims. They openly declare that their purposes can only be achieved by the forcible overthrow of the whole extant social order.

He later modified his views, or at least had doubts about the necessity of 'forcible overthrow', but apart from that the emphasis here is on struggling as an agent of history, and teaching. Notice incidentally, his remark that 'Communists scorn to hide their views and aims'. This is in striking contrast to Lenin's frequent references to the need for concealment and deception as a weapon of struggle. This difference goes to the root of the matter. Lenin's party needed concealment and deception because it was trying to mould, to influence, to wangle. Marx's party needed openness because it was trying to teach and because it was relying not on the party itself, but on the laws of history. If Communists hold or lose office in an organization, it does not matter much from a Marxist point of view. They can rely on the working of the laws of history. Indeed, for them to hold office when the organization did not accept their views, would be a disadvantage. It would confuse the picture and hold up the process of learning by the members. From the Leninist point of view, however, it matters a great deal that party members should hold office in organizations. From these key positions they can wangle the policy of the organization to fit in with general party policy at the time. Wangling organizations is part of trying to wangle history, but just for that reason it is not Marxist.

Indeed, there is nothing in Marxism which makes it necessary to have such a thing as *the* party. There can be several parties, each more or less on Marxist lines but differing in this or that respect. And the whole truth may not rest with any one of them. It will come out only as history unfolds.

I think I have said enough to show the anti-Marxist character of Leninist views of the party, and also something of what those Marxist views are and that they are sound. As Lucien Laurat points out in his book, *Marxism and Democracy*, in the section headed 'The Masses and the "Cadres"', Marxists like Rosa Luxemburg pointed out the Marxist theory of the leadership of the masses as opposed to the Leninist theory. I will quote from what Laurat has to say about Luxemburg's view. She points out, he says,

That in the socialist movement 'the relation between the masses and their leaders is reversed' as compared with the revolutionary movements of the past. The task of the leaders is no longer to impose their will upon the masses, but 'to enlighten the masses concerning their historic mission'. It is the masses themselves who must lead the movement with their own means, and their leaders are only 'the executive organs of the conscious action of the masses'. Rosa Luxemburg writes further in her polemic against Lenin: 'The only "subject" which the leaders of the movement today have to do with is the collective "I" of the working class, which resolutely demands the right to make its own mistakes, and to learn the dialectic of history by its own experience. And finally let us say bluntly that the mistakes committed by a really revolutionary working class movement are, historically, infinitely more fruitful and more valuable than the infallibility of the best Central Committee.'

However, she is well aware that the role which she assigns to the working class is in large measure an anticipation—not only for the Russian working class but also for the working class of Western Europe, because reality did not then correspond to that ideal. . . .

And Laurat goes on to comment:

So long as the working class has not achieved the necessary degree of maturity, the knowledge of 'the real aims of the struggle, its material content and its limits' must remain the property of a minority of leaders, and the reactions of the masses resemble those which characterised bourgeois revolutions. Hence came the Russian dilemma: to recognise frankly the lack of maturity of the masses, and advocate an organisation of a Jacobin-Blanquist type, thus turning one's back on Marxism, which is what Lenin did, or remain faithful to Marxist organisational principles, and try to create a democratic organisation, thus reducing the practical efficiency of the immediate action of the movement, which is what the Mensheviks did.

And finally:

The degree of democracy which exists in free working class organisations is the outcome of the given degree of enlightenment and maturity on the part of the masses, and this in itself, but not exclusively (there are other factors involved), is the outcome of the given degree of capitalist development.

There, that is genuine Marxism recognizing the operation of great historical forces including the proletariat, recognizing that the degree of development of the proletariat shapes working class parties and that these cannot be forces standing above history and moulding it.

Why Eastman should think that there is anything religious about recognizing laws of nature in history, I cannot imagine. Surely a scientific attitude to society requires that we should recognize that we can't do what we like with history, that, on the contrary, it has its own laws. It is the function of democratically-organized Marxist parties to expound those laws and to be the servants of progressive historical forces, not to try to be their masters.

CHAIRMAN: We all seem to be going in for long speeches. I suppose we'll have to give South his chance now. I hope you won't be too long-winded, South.

SOUTH: I'll do my best to be concise, Mr. Chairman. I am helped by the fact that I agree with what Allen has had to say in distinguishing Lenin's conception of the party from Marx's and also in pointing out Lenin's errors. So I'll concentrate on criticizing Marx's view.

First, I think Eastman is making a sound criticism when he describes Marx's view as religious, though this in no way justifies Lenin's approach. Allen is quite right when he repudiates Eastman's conception of social engineering. Society has its laws, its ways of working and it cannot be moulded or engineered by a political party except within narrow limits—certainly on nowhere near the scale Lenin attempted. Where we look back on a social change of a big character which was 'brought about' by a party, we find that appearances are deceptive, that the change was well under way before the party did anything about it, that the party in fact was thrown up and moulded by the same forces which were bringing about the change, that the party simply added a brick or two to a situation which was already largely developed. So far Allen is right and Eastman is wrong.

But Eastman is right about Marx because Marx went much further than that. Marx did not stop at saying that historical processes operate in accordance with their own laws. He regarded history as one process working to the classless society. It is this which justifies Eastman's criticism of Marx and which, unfortunately, obscures for Eastman what is sound in Marx as against Lenin, namely Marx's rejection of the Utopian approach which is simply another name for the engineering approach. You can engineer a bridge but you can't engineer a classless society. (And I might point out that you couldn't even engineer a sizeable bridge if you didn't have thousands of years of experience of successful dealing with similar problems, upon which to draw, whereas you have no experience whatever of the successful engineering of a classless society). These social engineers always take their problem extraordinarily cheaply, even if we waive the view that it would never be possible to engineer society in the way Lenin attempted.

However, let me leave Lenin right out of the picture and concentrate on the Marxist view of the party or parties. They are (a) democratically organized, (b) teachers of the proletariat, (c) when accepted by the proletariat as 'leaders', they carry out the will of the proletariat, (d) they join in all revolutionary movements against extant social and political conditions, (e) bring the property question to the fore in all situations, (f) scorn to hide their views and aims.

If society were moving in the direction of the classless society and if the proletariat were the class increasingly carrying on the struggle in this direction and becoming increasingly conscious of what they were doing, Marx's theory about the function of the Communists might work out. But in fact, these things are not happening. The workers are not showing increasing political activity and are not developing their own consciousness of what is happening. In the overwhelming majority they are not interested in the question of the direction in which society is moving. And among those few who are interested, neo-Leninist views (that is, Stalinist views), which are the product of a backward society and compatible only with backwardness, are the ones which win the most devoted adherents. Certainly there is very little development in a Marxist direction.

If a Marxist party tries to run itself democratically, then it remains a little isolated sect. And if by some stroke of fortune, by a coincidence of one of its demands with a popular demand, it secures a large influx of members, it soon ceases to be a Marxist party. And the Marxists within it are forced to get out and form themselves into a tiny splinter group again. Show me anywhere in the advanced countries of the world a mass Marxist Party. You cannot do it. And yet it is more than a hundred years since *The Communist Manifesto*. Surely this means that Marx was wrong. The workers are not doing what he expected them to do. (Incidentally, where you do find a Marxist party—I mean the real thing, not watered down versions that, despite lip-service to Marx, are really indistinguishable from our Labour Party—where you do find such a party, its members are as likely to be intellectuals as workers.)

I agree with Marx that the sort of party he speaks about would be the only sort appropriate to a genuine workers' struggle for liberation. But the great mass labour parties hold themselves together only by concentrating on day to day politics and immediate demands—in short, only by playing the Parliamentary game, the same as other Parliamentary parties—and by dodging the issues of interpretation, dodging the issue of consciousness. If one of them tried to raise that kind of issue, it would immediately split itself wide open. And outside those, we find only the splinter groups. So there is not a genuine workers' struggle for liberation—not on any significant scale.

The Communists who scorn to hide their views and aims (and they are few) by that very fact deprive themselves of worker support. They have taught the Marxist doctrine for a hundred years with such little success that even a plain and obvious false theory like Lenin's doctrine of the party can win more support than they can, and can even pass itself off in wide circles as *the* Marxist theory. So much for their role as teachers. It does not necessarily mean that they are bad teachers, not worse than most others at any rate, but it does mean that they are not getting the help they expected from History.

In other words, Marxist parties have got themselves into a historical blind alley. And I think this is due to the errors in Marxist predictions and to the errors in the Marxist analysis of society. The working class is not the political force they thought it would be. The working class can be used, has been used, and is being used to provide support for the policy of other social groups. Marxism provided those other social groups with an ideology which could be used to flatter the workers, make them seem important in their own eyes, and thereby hold their allegiance. Marx attributed an heroic historical role to the workers, but, in order to fulfil it, they would really have had to be heroic—intelligent, devoted, genuinely united, capable of enduring trials of understanding, physical strength, organizational and political capacity on the grand scale. But he did not mean to be flattering when he pointed this out. On the contrary, he said: You are not yet like this. You are not yet fit for your role. You will become fit only in the course of your struggle.

You can see how such a view could be used not for bracing to the task but for purposes of flattery to deflect from the task. If Marx had been right that would not have mattered, but he was wrong, and there is only the flimsiest social foundation nowadays for a genuinely Marxist party. If you doubt me, look about you.

If I might make a further point, I would say this: democratic organization and a theory of one historical path to a goal of a golden age do not go together. Any party which attempts to combine them has a deep contradiction at the heart of it. Democratic organization fits in with a pluralist outlook, with expecting the unexpected in the shifting complexities of political forces. A party can be democratically organized and can defend certain principles or ways of acting. It can say we don't know what challenges these principles will have to meet, we don't know what forces will attack them, or what forces in given situations will come to their defence. We don't know what organizational forms will be required from time to time. We will deal with these questions as they arise and in the spirit of our principles. Such an outlook is compatible with democracy. But when a party is founded upon a prediction of the course of the whole of history and of the role of one specific social class, then the tensions between this outlook and the democratic organization are great. There is the strong temptation to force history along the predicted path and, of course, this means forcing the party, abrogating the democracy within the party. I think that is a conflict within any Marxist Party which opens the way to the Leninist type of doctrine, though I fully admit that the Leninist type of doctrine is anti-Marxist.

CHAIRMAN: Thank you. South. That brings our discussions to an end.

Bibliography

ANDERSON, JOHN. 'Marxist Philosophy', Australasian Journal of Psychology and Philosophy, March 1935. Reprinted in *Studies in Empirical Philosophy*, Angus and Robertson, 1962.

BERKELEY, GEORGE. *Treatise Concerning the Principles of Human Knowledge* in *A New Theory of Vision and Other Writings*, London, Everyman Ed., 1954.

BUKHARIN, NIKOLAI. *Historical Materialism*, London, 1926.

EASTMAN, MAX. *Stalin's Russia and the Crisis in Socialism*, London, 1940.

——— *Marxism, is it Science?* London, 1941.

ENGELS, FRIEDRICH. Letter to J. Block in 1890, in Marx/ Engels, *Selected Works*, Moscow, 1962, Vol. 2.

——— Letter to C. Schmidt in 1890, in Marx/Engels, *Selected Works*, Moscow, 1962, Vol. 2.

——— Preface to Marx's *Civil War in France*, Marx/Engels *Selected Works*, Moscow, 1962, Vol. 1.

——— *Ludwig Feuerbach*, London, 1934. See also, Marx/ Engels, *Selected Works*, Moscow, 1962, Vol. 2.

——— Preface to Marx's *Class Struggles in France*, Marx/ Engels *Selected Works*, Moscow, 1962, Vol. 1.

——— *The Origin of the Family, Private Property and the State*, London, 1940. See also, Marx/Engels, *Selected Works*, Moscow, 1962, Vol. 2.

——— *Dialectics of Nature*, London, 1941.

——— *Anti-Duhring*, Third Ed., Moscow, 1962.

——— Speech at Marx's Grave, in Marx/Engels, *Selected Works*, Moscow, 1962, Vol. 2.

LAURAT, LUCIEN. *Marxism and Democracy*, London, 1940.

LENIN, VLADIMIR I. *What is to be Done?*, Collected Works, Moscow, 1960–70, Vol. 5.

———— *One Step Forward, Two Steps Back, Collected Works,* Moscow, 1960–70, Vol. 7.

———— *Materialism and Empirio-Criticism, Collected Works,* Moscow, 1960–70, Vol. 14.

———— *State and Revolution, Collected Works,* Moscow, 1960–70, Vol. 25.

———— *The Infantile Disease of Leftism, Collected Works,* Moscow, 1960–70, Vol. 31.

MARX, KARL. *The Civil War in France,* London, 1933, See also Marx/Engels, *Selected Works,* Moscow, 1962, Vol. 1.

———— *Critique of the Gotha Programme,* London, 1938. See also Marx/Engels, *Selected Works,* Moscow, 1962, Vol. 2.

———— Preface to *A Contribution to the Critique of Political Economy,* Marx/Engels, *Selected Works* Moscow, 1962, Vol. 1.

———— *The Eighteenth Brumaire of Louis Bonaparte,* Marx/Engels, *Selected Works,* Moscow, 1962, Vol. 1.

———— Letter to J. Weydemeyer, March, 1852, Marx/Engels, *Selected Works,* Moscow, 1962, Vol. 2.

———— *The Poverty of Philosophy,* Moscow, no date.

———— *The Holy Family,* Moscow, 1956.

———— *Introduction to a Critique of the Hegelian Philosophy of Right,* Marx/Engels, Collected Works, London, 1975–, Vol. 3.

MARX and ENGELS. *Manifesto of the Communist Party,* Marx/Engels, *Selected Works,* Moscow, 1962, Vol. 1.

———— *The German Ideology,* Moscow, 1965.

MORE, THOMAS. *Utopia,* London, 1901.

PLEKHANOV, GEORGE V. Preface to Engels *Socialism, Utopian and Scientific,* London, 1941.

———— *The Working Class and The Social Democratic Intelligentsia*

TROTSKY, LEON. *Terrorism and Communism,* Ann Arbor, Mich., 1961.

————. *The Revolution Betrayed,* Pathfinder, N.Y., 1970.

Index

Anderson, J., xvi, xvii, 12, quoted 14–15
Armed forces, 50
Avineri, S., xv
Axelrod, 109

Berkeley, G., 8; the subjectivist case, 5
Blanquist, 124, 143
Bolshevism, 134, 138, 140; dictatorship of proletariat, 122, 123, 124, 127, 129, 130; Luxemburg's criticism of, 129; Party, 139
Bonapartist, 53, 57
Bourgeoisie, xi, xii, 46, 64, 65, 103, 109, 124, 129, 134; economics, 62–3; ideology of, see Ideology; petty, 34, 35, 39, 42, 111; revolution, 36, 104–5, 113, 143; as workers, 111; see also Capitalism
Bukharin, N., 34

Capitalism, 23, 35, 36, 39, 42, 55–6, 91, 100, 111, 116, 118, 137; class interests of, 22, 25, 33, 34, 46, 48; as description of society, 99; dictatorship of, 51, 118, 119, 122; in Germany, 52; ideology of, see Ideology; international, 112; labour and,

xi, 63, 102–116 *passim*; restoration of, 118–19; and the State, 49, 53, 110, 126; see also Bourgeoisie
Causality, xiv, 8, 95
Christianity, xii, 22, 23, 24
Class, x, xi, 22, 25, 32, 33, 34, 46, 135, 137; Bourgeoisie, see Bourgeoisie; Capitalist, see Capitalism; development of new, 37; dissolution of, 106; divisions, 38; feudal, 36; ideology and, see Ideology; overthrow of, 36, 38; phases of, 34; as political units, 41, 109; relations, 40, 41, 43, 46; religion and, criticism, 76; ruling, 37–9, 43, 49, 50, 53, 65, 92, 106, 118; society, 34, 118; the State and, 46, 48, 54, 55; Theory of History, 32, 34, 40, 42, 46, 124, 141; Working class, see Proletariat, Workers
Class conflict, see Class struggle
Class struggle, xi, xiv, 32–44, 46, 101, 110, 111, 112, 145, 146; criticism of theory, 39–42, 68; dialectic of, 10, 68; and dictatorship of the proletariat, 124; laws of, 50; ownership of means of production, 33, 35; religion and, 41, 43; Scientific

---

* The name of Karl Marx occurs on almost every page of the text. To avoid unnecessary overloading, the entry under his name has been confined to the instances in which he is quoted and his works are mentioned.